Encounters

Moments of Destiny in the Bible

The majority of Biblical quotes are taken from the New International Version (NIV). Quotes from the Apocrypha are taken from the Revised Standard Version (RSV), and the story of Susanna from the New Revised Standard Version Catholic Edition (NRSVCE).

Translated by Cynthia Hindes

First published in German as
Das Buch der Fügungen: Schlüsselereignisse in der Bible
by Verlag Urachhaus, Stuttgart, in 2022
First published in English in 2023 by Floris Books, Edinburgh
© 2022 Verlag Freies Geistesleben & Urachhaus GmbH
English version © 2023 Floris Books
Ruth Ewertowski asserts her right under the Copyright, Designs and Patents Act 1988 to be recognised as the author of this Work

All rights reserved. No part of this publication
may be reproduced without prior permission
of Floris Books, Edinburgh
www.florisbook.co.uk

 Also available as an eBook

British Library CIP available
ISBN 978-178250-868-7

Encounters

Moments of Destiny in the Bible

Ruth Ewertowski

Contents

Foreword		7
1.	Herod and Nimrod: Hinderers Who Can Prevent Nothing	9
2.	At the Well: Hagar and the Angel; Rebekah and Isaac; Rachel and Jacob; Joseph	14
3.	Joseph: How Dreams Come True	21
4.	Joseph and Susanna: Dealing with Injustice	27
5.	Moses and His Mission: On the Way to Selfhood	32
6.	Moses Does Not Enter the Promised Land	37
7.	Rahab: Preparing the Way	43
8.	Samson: God-sent Yet Independent	49
9.	Ruth: The Stranger in Jesus' Family Tree	57
10.	Saul and the Necromancer: A King's End	63
11.	David: Fallible But Forgiven	69
12.	Job: The Rebellious Sufferer	75
13.	Judith: Pious Liberator or Temptress?	81
14.	Jonah the Initiate: Three Days in the Fish	88
15.	Tobias: Everything Falls into Place	94
16.	Daniel: A Loyalty Beyond the Reach of Power	100
17.	Dreams Change When Christ Appears	107
18.	Mary and Elizabeth	113
19.	The Birth of Jesus: Uniquely Atypical	120
20.	Moses and John: The Tragedy of the Forerunners	125
21.	Appearances of God	131

22.	Nicodemus: On the Threshold of a New Birth	137
23.	Christ and the Samaritan Woman	141
24.	Simon Peter: Courage and Weakness	147
25.	Why the Messiah is Also God's Servant	153
26.	Raising the Dead	159
27.	Christ's Experience of Powerlessness	165
28.	The Transformation of Hell	171
29.	Why Ascension Did Not Happen at Easter	177
30.	Pentecost	183
31.	What It Means to Heal a Lame Man	189
32.	Ananias and Sapphira: 'Why Has Satan Filled Your Heart?'	195
33.	Three Unlikely Baptisms	201
Endnotes		207
Bibliography		213

Foreword

When I'm asked what is on my mind at the moment, I am sometimes almost embarrassed to say biblical figures and stories. It sounds unworldly and does not fit into modern conversation. Nevertheless, it is a joy for me – though not always easy – to stand alongside the Old and New Testament figures and relive their encounters with each other and with God.

In the Bible, things do not happen in an orderly way. Events are always dazzling and far-fetched, yet something great and meaningful emerges from them. This applies even to guilty deeds, which become a supportive component of the story's meaning. They belong to the story's fulfilment even though we cannot justify them. Human freedom has an indispensable purpose: without it everything would be boringly providential.

By engaging with Bible stories, we can school ourselves in the old Greek philosophical concept of *paideia*: cultural education. One becomes more 'useful' knowing these stories.

The chapters of this book are revised essays that originally appeared in the journal *Die Christengemeinschaft* (The Christian Community). They can be read singly, but they also follow a course from background to fulfilment, from promise to realisation – though things usually turn out differently to what was expected.

Ruth Ewertowski

1. Herod and Nimrod: Hinderers Who Can Prevent Nothing

'Where is the newborn King of the Jews? We have seen his star in the east and have come to worship him.' (Matt. 2:2)

These words from the three wise men who had come to Jerusalem from the East struck fear into the heart of King Herod – he realised his power was under threat. Herod consulted with his advisors and they confirmed that the prince who would 'feed the people of Israel' would come from nearby Bethlehem. This had been foretold by the prophet Micah (Mic. 5:2). Herod met secretly with the three Magi (who later legends would declare to be kings) to find out what they knew about this newborn child who could depose him. Herod would not have learned much from them, but the Magi learned something from him, namely, where to look: in Bethlehem. That's where Herod sent them according to the prophecy. Herod also told the Magi to inform him as soon as they had found the child so that he, too, could go and pay homage.

The Magi set off again. The star that had been a sign to them of the birth of the new king had now become a wandering star, and it showed them where they had to go. They found the child and gave him what they had brought from afar – gold, frankincense, and myrrh. Each gift testified to Jesus' Messiahship – gold for the king, myrrh for the physician, and frankincense for the priest. He would be all of these in one person. It was to this that the three wise men from the East bowed. They were witnesses not in a legal sense but in the same way as John would be at the baptism of Jesus. Through their witnessing and their act of homage they declared Jesus' kingship: a kingship that only had power because it was a priestly and healing one. Thus, with their gifts, the three wise men had fulfilled their task.

However, the wise men were warned in a dream not to return to Herod, but to go back to their country by a different route. That dream saved Jesus' life. Mary's husband, Joseph, had a similar dream. He was commanded to flee with his family to Egypt and to remain there until Herod died.

Herod, realising that the wise men had betrayed him, reacted with all the violence and fury of a tyrant. Since he did not know which child threatened his rule, he ordered his soldiers to kill all boys two years old and younger.

We could easily take for granted Jesus' arrival in the world, yet it took place in the face of great obstacles and dangers. The question that the three wise men asked Herod, 'Where is the newborn king of the Jews?', unwittingly triggered an atrocity. For all their wisdom, the Magi did not see that the saviour sent from heaven would not be welcomed by someone so utterly obsessed with his own earthly power.

This is a shattering beginning. Many painters have shown the murderous event in all its brutality without being able to explain it. One stands, stunned, before the image of slaughtered innocent children with which Jesus' path towards Christ's act of redemption begins. Today, the murder of those innocents is doubted; it is considered a fiction, a case of poetic license because there is

1. HEROD AND NIMROD

no historical evidence for the killing. On the other hand, early theologians such as Saint Augustine and Saint Caesarius of Arles glorified the event because the murdered children were granted martyrdom for dying for Jesus. Both possibilities only show how difficult it is to interpret an atrocity. We are challenged to go beyond the alternatives of either proof or glorification.

Something quite different appears if we see the story as a type of narrative, one that has historical antecedents. If we turn to the Old Testament we find that Herod has a little-known predecessor, a legendary forerunner about whom one can also ask what is fiction and what is truth. In the end, these questions are not the ones that matter. What is essential is the power of the narrative and the way in which meaning appears despite all human catastrophes, a meaning that asserts itself without justifying the events themselves.

In the Old Testament, the Babylonian ruler Nimrod could be seen as Herod's forerunner. Legend, as well as Jewish and Islamic traditions, suggest he is a Herodian character. In Genesis we read that Nimrod had gained power on Earth (Gen. 10:8), placing himself above others, independent of God's rule. He was said to have inspired the building of the Tower of Babel. Islamic tradition knows him as a tyrant who allowed himself to be worshipped as a god. Sura 21 of the Koran states that it was Nimrod who had Abraham/Ibrahim thrown into a fire, from which he was miraculously rescued.

According to one legend, Nimrod learned through a dream or special position of the stars that a child would be born in his city of Ur who would destroy all idols and dethrone worldly rulers. Rudolf Steiner also referred to this legend in his lectures on the Gospel of Matthew.[1] In another version, it was a star that, according to the astrologers, represented an evil omen and heralded the birth of a child who would destroy Nimrod's power.[2] Nimrod then ordered

Terah, one of his commanders, to kill all newborn sons. But Terah was also expecting the birth of a child. To protect his wife and their unborn baby, Terah hid them in a cave. There, Terah's wife gave birth to Abraham, the first patriarch and the one with whom Jesus' line of ancestors begins in Matthew's Gospel. Abraham escaped, just as Jesus would later escape Herod's preemptive murders.

Abraham grew up in the cave, where he would stay until he was seven years old (or perhaps only three). He was nourished by an angel who let him suck milk from its fingertips. Rudolf Steiner explains that one of the peculiarities of Abraham's early childhood years (perhaps due to living in the cave) was that those forces that otherwise manifest themselves in clairvoyant abilities instead influenced Abraham's ability to think. His brain was formed physically in such a way that he was able to think the concept 'God'. Abraham also developed logical thinking, which is why the beginnings of mathematics are attributed to him. That ability, bound to the physical brain, could only be passed on through heredity. From Abraham there descended a series of generations that culminated in the birth of the Solomon Jesus, the child described in the Gospel of Matthew. This child stood at the end of an evolution and, just like his ancestor Abraham at the beginning, he was threatened by a terrible danger.

Nimrod and Herod were stumbling blocks to Christ's incarnation, hinderers who could prevent nothing, and neither were they alone. The long prehistory of Christ is filled with astonishing dangers. Again and again one has the impression that everything could have gone wrong, and yet things turned out entirely differently. Abraham remained childless into old age and then nearly sacrificed the child he finally had with Sarah. With some of the dangers, one may wonder whether God staged them, but infanticide cannot be reconciled with God. And what would have

1. HEROD AND NIMROD

happened if Abraham had not been willing to sacrifice his beloved son Isaac? Could he even have become Jesus' ancestor without that purification? It all makes Christ's incarnation seemingly impossible. And yet at the same time, it is just this impossible incarnation that very subtly and delicately becomes a reality. There is much that is difficult to grasp, but it is just through all this that Christ becomes so particularly real.

2. At the Well: Hagar and the Angel; Rebekah and Isaac; Rachel and Jacob; Joseph

Wells are places where history is written. In the Old Testament, a little-known woman had an encounter at a well that had extraordinary meaning for the future. The woman's name was Hagar. She was the Egyptian maidservant of Abraham's wife, Sarah, who was childless at the time. Because of this, and with Sarah's consent (even at her request), Abraham conceived a child with Hagar. The happiness of promptly becoming pregnant and being able to give Abraham a child, led to Hagar feeling superior to her mistress. In response, Sarah began to treat her maidservant harshly.

Afraid, Hagar fled into the desert. There, the angel of the Lord met her at a watering spring and announced the imminent birth of a son. Hagar was to name him Ishmael and he would become a patriarch (Gen. 16:7–16). He would be a wild man, defiant, but he would live with his brothers, that is with Abraham's children who at that time had not been born. Like Jacob later on, Ishmael would become the father of twelve tribes and his descendants would be great (Gen. 25:12–18). Ishmael was considered the ancestor of the Arabs, and Islam counts him among its prophets.

Hagar, who found herself enviously disregarded by her mistress, felt recognised by God. She said of the God who appeared to her in the form of an angel, 'You are the God who sees me' (Gen. 16:13),

2. AT THE WELL

and the well where that happened was given the name Beer-Lahai-Roi, which means 'the well of the Living One who sees me'. Hagar was encouraged by the God who saw her, and she could then follow his command to return to her mistress.

Thus, Ishmael grew up with his father. He was thirteen years old when God made a covenant with Abraham and announced the birth of Abraham's second son, this time by his wife Sarah, who by now was ninety years old. His name would be Isaac, and though second-born, he would take the place of the first-born Ishmael, just as Isaac's son Jacob would later take the place of his first-born son, Esau.

One can be amazed at the complicated paths God's story takes with his chosen people. It is never what one expects. Who can blame Sarah for laughing when she learned that she would become a mother at her age? On the one hand, both prophecy and promise come true, and yet on the other, again and again, there is the impact of the new and completely unexpected.

Abraham, the progenitor of Israel, who only narrowly escaped Nimrod's infanticide, had to deal with this. It constituted and increased the intensity of his relationship with God. At God's command, Abraham was prepared to sacrifice his son, Isaac, the one on whom the future people of God depended. Everything was about to dissolve into nothing. But Abraham's submission to the will of God established his reliability. He became a sort of Peter, as it were, the rock and foundation for the chosen people's prosperity.

Shortly before his death, Abraham wanted a wife found for his son, Isaac, who was born a second time on the altar of sacrifice. It was considered an urgent matter because Isaac was then about forty years old. Abraham appointed his senior servant, presumably Eliezer, to find a suitable bride from Abraham's homeland so that his people would not turn to foreign gods. The servant traveled to Mesopotamia, and in the region of Haran he stopped at a well with his ten camels. He knew that the women from the surrounding villages would come here in the evening to draw water. Perhaps the woman he was looking for would be among them.

But how would he be able to find the right woman for Isaac? In prayerful conversation with the God of Abraham, the servant laid down the criterion that this woman had to fulfil:

> Lord, God of my master Abraham, make me successful today, and show kindness to my master Abraham. See, I am standing beside this spring, and the daughters of the townspeople are coming out to draw water. May it be that when I say to a young woman, 'Please let down your jar that I may have a drink,' and she says, 'Drink, and I'll water your camels too,' let her be the one you have chosen for your servant Isaac. By this I will know that you have shown kindness to my master. (Gen. 24:12–14)

An answer could not have been quicker in coming. Even before the suitor had finished speaking, a beautiful young woman came with a pitcher on her shoulder, which she filled at the well. At the servant's request for water, she gave him a drink and without further ado said, 'I'll draw water for your camels too.' She did not rest until all had water. The woman was Rebekah, granddaughter of Nahor, who was Abraham's brother. Everything happens in this story with such certainty of purpose and coherence that even Rebekah's father and brother could only say to Abraham's servant, 'This is from the Lord; we can say nothing to you one way or the other. Here is Rebekah; take her and go. Let her become the wife of your master's son, as the Lord has directed' (Gen. 24:50–51).

God had decided; but it was not a strange decision, like Isaac's sacrifice demanded of Abraham. At the well, things ran more

2. AT THE WELL

fluidly than one could imagine. Guidance, providence and human self-determination came into perfect harmony there. Yes, even the mind is fully satisfied, for what bride could be more suitable in her beauty, virginity, and kindness than the one who also acted pragmatically? She not only gave water to Abraham's servant but also cared for his animals. All the conditions were fulfilled, and simultaneously they allow a glimpse into the heart of the young woman we hardly recognise in the older Rebekah. Later she would spin an intrigue to put her favourite son Jacob in place of Isaac's favourite first-born son. But now, everything that was feminine in the best sense of the word, the drawing, the giving, the caring, came to fruition in the setting of the well. The next morning, Rebekah set out with Abraham's servant to meet her unknown bridegroom, Isaac.

Rudolf Frieling writes that for Abraham and Jacob trees and stones play a decisive role. Abraham meets the three archangels at the Oak Grove of Mamre. Jacob uses a stone to mark the place where he has a vision of angels going up and down a ladder leading to heaven. Isaac, however, is a man of wells.[1] He went to the 'well of the Living One who sees me'. He would live at that well, revive buried wells and dig new ones. At the well where Hagar knew God saw her, he met his future wife for the first time, who was brought to him by his father's servant. At the well, things happened with God's approval, quickly and with the best of outcomes: Abraham's servant had just explained what he had arranged. 'Then Isaac brought her [Rebekah] into the tent of Sarah, his mother, and took Rebekah, and she became his wife, and he loved her.' (Gen. 24:67).

As quickly and smoothly as all that went, Isaac had to wait a long time for offspring, for, despite her suitability as a wife in all other respects, Rebekah proved infertile. Only after twenty years of marriage and Isaac's fervent prayer did Rebekah give birth to twins who already in her womb struggled for precedence. Before the birth, God had prophesied to her that the older would serve the younger. Later, she helped Jacob, the younger, receive Isaac's blessing. If Isaac thought in dying that he was blessing Esau, his first-born, he was deceived. Jacob and his mother fulfilled a divine promise. And yet they did so through a deception for which they both had to atone – they did not see each other again. Jacob had to flee from his brother's revenge and would not return for twenty-one years. By then, Rebekah was no longer alive.

Jacob would fulfil prophecies. The twelve tribes of Israel would descend from him, and yet at the same time this arose out of a sacrilegious act. Once more, it would be a well where fate was decided.

Following his mother's advice, Jacob went to his uncle Laban. Just before he reached his destination, he came to a well. It must have been a different well from the one where Abraham's servant found Rebekah, for it was covered with a stone that had to be rolled away. This required the combined strength of all the shepherds, and since not all were gathered yet Jacob had to wait. It was at the well that Jacob first set eyes on Rachel. In his book *Joseph and His Brothers*, Thomas Mann describes that moment: 'Then he saw her first, his heart's destiny, the bride of his soul, around whose eyes he was to serve fourteen years, the lamb's ewe.'[2] The lamb Rachel would bear (her name means 'ewe' in Hebrew), and for whom Jacob would have to wait many years, would be Joseph.

The first encounter between Jacob and Rachel, which owed itself to his escape after a deception rich in blessings, must have been powerful. It gave Jacob the strength to roll away the stone in front of the well on his own and then water all his uncle Laban's sheep. The most natural course of events that once made Rebekah draw water for Abraham's servant who had come looking for a bride

2. AT THE WELL

for Isaac, similarly connected Jacob with his future wife. But then things took an unexpected turn and Jacob the cheat was himself deceived.

According to his agreement with Laban, Jacob was allowed to marry Laban's daughter after seven years. However, on the wedding night, Laban brought his eldest daughter, Leah, to Jacob who only recognised her in the morning. 'Why have you done this to me?' Jacob asked his father-in-law. Laban replied by insisting on the proper order of siblings, which Jacob had so thoroughly disregarded in his own actions towards Esau. It was not customary in that land 'to give the younger daughter in marriage before the older one' (Gen. 29:26). Jacob eventually married Rachel after another seven years of work. But that first wedding night with Leah rather than Rachel, seemed to serve as a counterpoint to Isaac's blessing of Jacob when Isaac thought he was consecrating Esau. Thus, the spirit of history seems to have restored a balance.

What was also repeated was the infertility of the beloved woman. As with Sarah and Rebekah, Rachel's son, the lamb of the ewe, was a long time coming. But he came, the one long yearned for and preferred by Jacob above all others. It was Joseph through whom the twelve tribes of Israel would come to Egypt (again via a well story) only to be led out of that land almost five hundred years later by Moses.

Joseph's experience with a well differed from finding a bride. The well itself was also quite different: it was dried up, not a source of life but a place of death. Joseph first had to die before he could really live. Jacob would sacrifice his beloved son, although unlike Abraham he would do so involuntarily. But once again, this would bring about a turning point in his people's destiny.

Jacob's favouritism towards Joseph, as well as Joseph's smug behaviour, aroused his brothers' envy. Prompted by a kind of clueless narcissism, Joseph told his brothers that he had dreamed they would one day bow down before him. In response to this, his brothers threw him into a dry well from which they subsequently freed him so they could sell him to a caravan of merchants heading for Egypt. Joseph, the dreamer with a complacently self-confident sense of mission, emerged from his well-grave in a way that allowed him to accept and cope almost humbly with all his trials in Egypt. His dreams would be fulfilled, but for that to happen they first had to be forgotten.

It was Joseph who, with wise foresight, made provision during the seven fat years for the seven lean ones that Pharaoh had dreamt of in coded form. When Joseph's brothers, driven by hunger, came to Egypt's full granaries to buy grain, they met Pharaoh's representative and bowed before him. They did not recognise their brother Joseph, but Joseph recognised them. He remembered his dreams, which had finally come true. After many years, Joseph had become one before whom the brothers could bow; it had been impossible with the seventeen-year-old dreamer he had been.

With Joseph, his experience in the well became an initiation into life. The dried-up well was not a drinking trough but a place of transformation that must first be mastered.

3. Joseph: How Dreams Come True

Jacob's preference for Joseph over his eleven brothers, the promotion of his vanity through the gift of a 'many-coloured coat', and Joseph's dreams in which he saw himself adored by his brothers, meant that a reversal of fortune was almost inevitable. An intervention was needed.

If a seventeen-year-old dreamt that the sheaves of grain that his brothers were binding bowed down before his own, and if he dreamt that the sun, moon and stars bowed down before him, and he could not keep these things to himself, it was no wonder that he made enemies of his brothers. His father criticised him for his arrogance (Gen. 37:10), but instead of teaching him the necessary humility, he sent Joseph to where his brothers were tending the flocks to see 'if all is well' with them (37:14). One can imagine how their unrest grew when Joseph arrived in his colourful coat and, as Thomas Mann puts it in his novel, says to them, 'Yes, yes, greetings! Trust your eyes, dear men! I have come on my father's account on Hulda, the donkey, to look after you.'[1]

That was the final straw. They couldn't tolerate any more of Joseph's arrogant behaviour and they decided to kill him – at least then his self-important dreams wouldn't come true. It was Reuben, the eldest brother, who intervened to save Joseph's life. Rather than spilling his blood, he suggested they throw him into an empty well close by. They stripped him of his precious coat and threw him naked into the well. When a caravan of Ishmaelite merchants passed by, Joseph's brother Judah saw an opportunity to get rid of him at a profit without incurring any blood guilt. They pulled him out of the well and sold him to the Ishmaelites. Then they took his coat, soaked it in goat's blood and took it back to their father who, heartbroken, concluded that his darling son was dead.

Being thrown naked into a pit, a prison, or a grave is a situation reminiscent of death. Joseph got a taste of it. That was his first humiliation. The second came when the Ishmaelites arrived in Egypt and sold Joseph to Potiphar, a high royal dignitary. Joseph was now a slave. No one was bowing down before him, not his brothers, not the stars or the sun or the moon. No one. He was at the bottom.

But from those depths, Joseph worked his way up. Potiphar soon realised how prudent and reliable he was, and he left Joseph in charge of his household. Joseph did not take advantage of his position; he knew where he belonged. When Potiphar's wife wanted Joseph to be her lover, he remained steadfast in the face of her seduction. Humiliated, Potiphar's wife took revenge on him just as his brothers had done. Having snatched his cloak as Joseph fled her advances, Potiphar's wife used it as 'proof' that he had attempted to force himself on her, fleeing only when she screamed for help. As a result, Joseph went to prison for something he did not do. This was the third humiliation.

But again, Joseph proved skillful and trustworthy. The prison bailiff, like Potiphar, left all his house business to him. Here, the dreams that had been his undoing back home proved a decisive help. Joseph interpreted the dreams of two fellow prisoners, the former chief baker and the former chief cupbearer of Pharoah.

3. JOSEPH: HOW DREAMS COME TRUE

He foretold death by hanging for the chief baker, and release from prison and reinstatement in office for the chief cupbearer. Both events came to pass. When the cupbearer was released, Joseph asked him to intercede on his behalf with Pharaoh, but the cupbearer forgot all about him.

Joseph remained a prisoner for two years. It was a long period of inner change and growth. Then, once again, dreams led to a reversal in his fortunes. Pharaoh had two dreams that no one could interpret for him. In one, seven lean cows devoured seven fat ones, and in the other, seven thin ears of corn consumed seven full and thick ones. Although they seemed to bode ill, no one knew what they meant. Finally, the cupbearer remembered the man who had correctly interpreted his dream. Pharaoh sent for Joseph.

Joseph's hour had come. Freshly coiffed and dressed, he stood before the greatest of the world. When Pharaoh said that he had heard Joseph could interpret dreams, Joseph replied, 'I cannot do it, but God will give Pharaoh the answer he desires' (41:16). Modest but certain, he announced that God was on Pharaoh's side even before he knew the dreams.

Pharaoh told Joseph his dreams and Joseph interpreted them clearly and decisively. After seven years of plenty, he told Pharaoh, there would follow seven years of famine. But that was no reason to despair, for in the years of plenty one could make provisions for the famine so that no one would go hungry. God sent Pharaoh the dreams so that he would be able to make those provisions. It was just a matter of finding the right man to lead the efforts. Joseph interpreted the dreams so convincingly and with such practicality that Pharaoh was immediately sure he had found his man. After enduring the pit, slavery and prison, Joseph became Pharaoh's deputy, the second most important man in Egypt. What looked like a steep career ascent had behind it some thirteen years of quiet maturing. His task was to ensure that the Egyptian people survived the difficult times ahead; it was an enormous responsibility. Joseph would have to show that he had earned Pharaoh's trust.

Joseph would indeed show that he was the man he had dreamed of as a seventeen-year-old boy, the one before whom others would bow. But he could only become that man because he had experienced the hardships brought on by those very dreams, hardships which at the time had seemed so unjust. That is what is unique about Joseph's story, his destiny, mistakes and success. His dreams foretold what was to come, yet for them to be fulfilled Joseph had to walk a path through the abyss. That alone allowed him to become the man for whom those dreams came into effect. His brothers would indeed bow down before him in the end. But fulfilling those dreams along a path of initiation challenged him severely.[2]

Joseph was about thirty years old when he entered Pharaoh's service, and it would be another seven years before he saw his brothers again. First came the seven years of plenty, followed by the predicted famine for which Joseph took the proper precautions.

During the time of abundance, two sons were born to him to whom he gave names indicative of his life situation. He named his first-born Manasseh, which means 'to forget', because he said, 'God has made me forget all my misfortune and all my father's household' (41:51). That did not mean that everything was erased from his memory, but that Joseph was able to let go of all loss and hurt.

He called his second son Ephraim, which means 'doubly fruitful' because 'God has made me fruitful in the land of my suffering' (41:52). Joseph was a gifted man and a man of success. But grace was not a bed of roses. In it lay the weight of the mandate to overcome oneself. The names of his sons denoted Joseph's grace and struggle: his ability to forgive and his ability to create.

3. JOSEPH: HOW DREAMS COME TRUE

The years of famine were coming and distress gripped all the lands. 'And all the world came to Egypt to buy from Joseph' (41:57). The sons of Israel, Joseph's brothers, came and fell down before him. Joseph immediately recognised them and thought of his old dreams. However, he did not make himself known to them but first put them to the test. They, too, had to go through steps of initiation until they could be reconciled. Joseph accused them of being spies and they had to justify themselves and show who they had become over the years.

Because Benjamin, Joseph's only full brother, was not with them, he kept one of the brothers, Simeon, as a hostage to see whether they would stand by each other and redeem Simeon. Reluctantly, Jacob let Benjamin, who was his favourite after Joseph was presumed dead, go with them. On their second visit, they bowed and fell before Joseph. When they did that a third time, the test would be complete.

Joseph secretly had his silver cup packed in Benjamin's sack with the grain he had bought, so that he might capture him as a fugitive thief. Knowing that losing Benjamin would be their father's certain death, the brothers fell to the ground before Joseph for the last time (44:14). Judah, whose idea it had been to sell Joseph to the Ishmaelite merchants all those years ago, gave a long and courageous speech in which he offered himself as a slave in exchange for Benjamin. He could not abide the misery that would come upon Jacob if he lost his second beloved as well (44:34). That was enough; Joseph recognised his brothers' righteousness. They, too, had walked a path of probation and thus reconciliation was possible. Joseph revealed himself to his frightened brothers. The sentence, 'Only trust your eyes, dear men!' would be appropriate. It was he, and he was a kind of risen Christ for them. The situation bears anticipatory features of the Mystery of Golgotha.

The brothers were forgiven, for they did not know what they were doing when they betrayed and sold Joseph:

> And now, do not be distressed and do not be angry with yourselves for selling me here, because it was to save lives that God sent me ahead of you ... to preserve for you a remnant on Earth and to save your lives by a great deliverance. (45:5–7)

God had changed the evil intentions of men. That did not mean that evil was a prerequisite for the good, but that it came about differently from what human judgment considered possible. 'You intended to harm me,' said Joseph, completely reconciled at the very end of his great story, 'but God intended it for good to accomplish what is now being done, the saving of many lives' (50:20).

One might expect Joseph's two sons to become the forefathers of the tribe from which Jesus of Nazareth emerged. But that did not happen. Instead, Perez, one of the twin sons that Judah so improperly begot with his daughter-in-law Tamar, became an ancestor of Jesus. And Judah, who at first behaved so questionably, then became a worthy bearer of Jesus' family tree in his willingness to sacrifice himself for Benjamin before Joseph. Judah and Tamar's indelicate story was inserted into Joseph's story just after the passage that told of Joseph's sale to the Ishmaelites (Gen. 38). Here, the die was already cast for the future of Israel, which would culminate in the incarnation of Christ.

All these stories are so wonderfully intertwined that all planning and calculation must fall silent before the brilliant author of the great story.

4. Joseph and Susanna: Dealing with Injustice

When Jacob's son Joseph was sold to Egypt, he came to live in the house of Potiphar, a high royal dignitary considered a eunuch. Joseph proved to be a great organiser and Potiphar soon placed the running of his house entirely in Joseph's hands, caring for nothing more than his own food and drink. Potiphar's wife took a liking to the busy and handsome Joseph and invited him to lie with her. But Joseph, who by now was in no way inferior to Potiphar in rank, refused her. Another man's wife was taboo for him because adultery was a sin against God. After many futile efforts to win him over, the frustrated wife's love for Joseph turned to hatred. When, in a last attempt to bring him to her bed Joseph fled from her, she accused him of attempted rape. As proof, she held up his garment which she had snatched from him as he ran away. Potiphar had Joseph taken prisoner, indeed he was lucky that he was not killed. As a result of this Joseph ended up in Pharaoh's prison, and this set the stage for his momentous encounter with Pharaoh later on.

~

The female counterpart to Joseph is Susanna, who lived in exile in Babylon. Her story is recorded in the Greek translation of the Book of Daniel in two versions, the Septuagint and the Theodotion.

It is not found in the Aramaic/Hebrew version of the Book of Daniel. Its more detailed, possibly later version is the Theodotion, named after the Hellenistic Jewish scholar who translated the Old Testament into Greek in the second century AD. It prevailed over the Septuagint and was the basis of Luther's translation, but it appears there only as an addition to the Book of Daniel preceding it. In more modern versions, such as the Catholic edition of the New Revised Standard Version quoted throughout this chapter, Susanna's story appears as the thirteenth chapter at the end of the Book of Daniel.

Susanna was the beautiful wife of the rich and respected Joakim, whose majestic house was often used as a meeting place for Jews. Among them were two elders who had been appointed as judges and who decided disputes at Joakim's house. During their visits, these two men repeatedly observed the beautiful woman who liked to spend time in her garden. Desire grew in them and made them foolish (Dan. 13:9, NRSVCE).

One of the elders, unaware that the other shared his desire for Susanna, said, 'Come, let us go home, for it is now time to eat.' They left the garden and went their separate ways, only for both men to return shortly after to the place they had just left. Such an embarrassing encounter might have served to bring them to their senses, but instead it led them to formulate a plan to obtain the object of their desire. The judges were now clearly on the path of injustice as they waited for an opportunity. It arose when Susanna came into the garden to bathe and sent her maids away to bring her oil and ointments. The maids had locked the garden so that no unauthorized person could enter, but the two elders were already hiding within. They approached Susanna, harassed her and threatened to accuse her of adultery with a young man if she did not do their bidding.

4. JOSEPH AND SUSANNA: DEALING WITH INJUSTICE

Susanna remained steadfast and refused the two old men. She cried out to defend herself, but they turned the situation against her and testified before Joakim and all the people. 'While we were walking in the garden alone, this woman came in with two maids, shut the garden doors and dismissed the maids. Then a young man, hiding there, came and lay with her' (Dan. 13:36, NRSVCE). The two elders claimed they could not overpower the young man but were able to overcome the adulterous woman whom they convicted of a crime. The evidence was compelling. The two elders were believed and Susanna was sentenced to death. Evil seemed to triumph over good.

But Susanna, unlike Joseph, turned to God with a loud voice. Only God could know the hidden truth, but at least the others heard her prayer. And her prayer was answered. A young man appeared. But this was not someone who would lead Susanna to her doom, for it was said that in this man God had awakened his Holy Spirit.

'I want no part in shedding this woman's blood!' he cried to the crowd (Dan. 13:46, NRSVCE).

The young man's name was Daniel. His name means 'God provides justice', and that is just what happened. In separate interrogations Daniel proved that the two old men were lying. They named completely different trees under which they claimed to have seen the alleged adultery, and it also became clear that the judges had repeatedly bent the law in their judgments. The supposed wisdom of the judges was replaced by a method that was logical and comprehensible to all, thereby introducing into legal life the principle of independent questioning of witnesses that is still used today. Daniel saved Susanna's life and the two elders were led away to face their death sentence. Right had triumphed and, as if in a concluding choral song, the people with loud voices praised God 'who saves those who hope in him' (Dan. 13:61, NRSVCE).

Did Joseph not trust in God when he was falsely accused? Should he have cried out and hoped for a testimony of his innocence? Why did he remain silent? Why did Joseph not complain to the merchants? He let himself be sold by his brothers and taken to Egypt without a word, and without complaint he innocently went to Pharaoh's prison.

However, to question why Susanna protests and Joseph remains silent is ultimately to miss the spirit of the narrative that is inherent in both stories, though in very different ways.

The story of Susanna is a teacher's narrative. It makes a statement that could also have been made with a philosophical-theological text. The 'moral of the story' is that the wicked are punished and that virtue and trust in God are rewarded. It encourages the reader to follow Susanna's example in a comparable situation, trusting in God and holding fast to the law. Furthermore, her story, especially in cases where it precedes the book of Daniel, may even have had the function of announcing Daniel as divinely inspired and thus as a prophet.

In the case of Joseph, on the other hand, it makes little sense to speak of the story's function or moral. It is not an instructional narrative. No theology or doctrine is developed. It is instead a work of art. Its overall context reveals meaning without maxims for action being derived from it. Destiny unfolds with the participants helping to shape it out of their freedom, even though they are unable to fully comprehend it in all its detail and meaning.

Joseph's brothers may have taken revenge on him by selling him to the Midianite merchants, just as Potiphar's wife did later when she falsely accused him of rape because of he rejected her, but Joseph himself was no paragon of virtue. He did not single-mindedly pursue any kind of career, and yet quite an astonishing career unfolded for him nevertheless. He became, after Pharaoh, the most powerful man in all of Egypt, responsible for helping its people through a great famine. Joseph's father and brothers would have become victims had Joseph not found his way into that position through felicitously unfortunate circumstances.

Joseph revealed himself to his unsuspecting brothers, who appeared before him as supplicants. But that scene has a different revelatory character than the one in which Daniel proves Susanna's innocence. Joseph's story is not about finding the truth by uncovering a lie that needs to be punished. The story is not on the level of legality. It is life as a work of art in which a different morality prevails.

Nor is it a matter of an active or passive relationship that results from a condition of will. It is a relationship of magnanimity, forgiveness and trust. After Jacob died, Joseph's brothers were afraid that out of grief for their father he might repay them for all the evil they had once done him. As a precaution, they fell before him and said, 'Behold, we are your servants.' But Joseph said to them, 'Fear not! Am I then standing in the place of God? You intended to harm me, but God intended it for good to accomplish what is now being done, the saving of many lives' (Gen. 50:18–20). Circumstances and events unfolded differently from what their human actors had intended. They were woven together both through and despite their intentions.

The Susanna narrative has its meaning on a different level, namely on the level of justice, which was finally granted because God intervened for an innocent victim accused in a hopeless situation. God had provided justice through Daniel, whose name indicated such assistance; human beings participated in that justice. With the story of Joseph, however, we enter the sphere of meaningful destiny in which morality is to be sought more in attitudes than in actions.

5. Moses and His Mission: On the Way to Selfhood

Moses, one of the most important personalities of the Judeo-Christian religion, got his name from his adoptive Egyptian mother, Pharaoh's daughter. 'Moses' in Egyptian meant 'child of' or 'son of' – for example, Thutmoses, which means 'child of Thoth'. In this case it meant son of an unknown father. In Hebrew, the name stands for 'extractor', perhaps transformed from 'extracted' since Moses was pulled out of the Nile. That transformation was like an unintended prophecy because the one who was pulled out became the one who pulled the people of Israel out of Egypt.[1] In a sense, Moses was born several times and was himself the midwife of his people. Thus, his naming by his adoptive mother was confirmed even after the fact.

Moses was born about four hundred years after Jacob's favourite son, Joseph, had died. Although the people of Israel came to Egypt with Joseph and lived there for a long time in peace and prosperity, these conditions had changed significantly by Moses' time. Joseph's services to Egypt were forgotten, and the friendly relations between the two peoples had become hostile. The Israelites were compelled to work on public buildings; overseers were put in charge of them, and their work became slavery (Exod. 1:11–14).

The Israelites had become so numerous that the Egyptians perceived them as an internal threat. They tried to keep them

5. MOSES AND HIS MISSION

down through slavery, and when that failed Pharaoh resorted to yet another means: infanticide. It was not the soldiers who did the slaughtering, as Herod's would later, rather *all* Egyptians were called upon to throw newborn Israelite sons into the Nile. But just as Nimrod's infanticide order could not thwart Abraham, and just as Herod could not kill Jesus, Pharaoh could not impede the one who would make Israel self-sufficient. Indeed, the whole Egyptian army would be destroyed eighty years later in its attempt to stop Israel from leaving Egypt – during their pursuit, the army would drown in the Sea of Reeds.

There are always outstanding moments in human history when exactly the opposite happens of what was intended. In these moments of circumvention and defeat, the spirit of history comes into play in its own unique way. These are junctures of development when something new breaks through. In the figure of Moses this happens with an epic slowness that corresponds to the time span of the Old Testament, which moves in decades and centuries.

A man and a woman from the house of Levi had a son who was not killed because three months after his birth, his mother placed him in a waterproof reed basket on the Nile.[2]

Of all people, the daughter of the Pharaoh who ordered the infanticide discovered that basket and took care of the boy lying inside. He was a Hebrew woman's son. Pharaoh's daughter knew that and thus acted against her father out of compassion. She may not have known that Moses' sister had been closely following his journey down the Nile so that Pharaoh's daughter could find a wet nurse who would breastfeed the child, namely Moses' biological mother. And so it happened that Moses spent the first four years of his life in the bosom of his family. Then his sister brought him back to Pharaoh's daughter, probably following an appointment, where he would remain for the time being. Until he reached adulthood,

Moses was fed and educated in the house of the one who wanted to kill him. 'Moses was taught all the wisdom of the Egyptians,' says the Acts of the Apostles (Acts 7:22), and he had the prospect of succeeding Pharaoh himself one day. Moses became an Egyptian.

But then everything changed. As did Buddha centuries later, Moses had lived in great comfort and prosperity far from worldly suffering. And, like Buddha, on his first foray into the world beyond the one he knew, he immediately witnessed suffering. He saw the enslavement of the Hebrews and the violence of their Egyptian oppressors. In an act of vigilante justice, Moses slew an Egyptian overseer who had mistreated a Hebrew worker. Moses did so with some deliberation, for he looked around beforehand and buried the dead man afterwards. However, Moses found no solidarity among his Hebrew 'brethren'. He punished the injustice of the oppressors but then could not find justice among the oppressed, who also beat each other.

Moses' deed had not gone unobserved and he was forced to flee from Pharaoh. But just because of this, he would reach the place where he would finally receive his mission. At Horeb, the mountain of God, he would be called to free the people of Israel from Egypt, to found a new culture, and enter into a new relationship with God.

After his escape, Moses came to the land of Midian. He was around forty years old. In Midian he helped the seven daughters of the local priest Jethro (sometimes also called Reguel or Reuel, meaning 'friend of God') water their father's sheep at a well. He married one of these daughters and had two sons. The first he named Gershom, meaning 'stranger there', which expressed his attitude to life: 'I have become a stranger in a strange land' (Exod. 2:22). Moses was the son without a father, a stranger who had to settle in the land of Midian.

And then nothing happened for a long time.

5. MOSES AND HIS MISSION

In time, Moses overcame his foreignness. He settled into his life as a shepherd, tending his father-in-law's sheep, and things could have carried on like that indefinitely. Who would have expected anything else after such a long time? But after forty years in hiding, Moses received his real mission. He was now eighty.

Moses was looking after his father-in-law's flock when he came to Mount Horeb, which was connected to the God of Israel in a special way. There he saw a thorn bush engulfed in fire, but the bush did not burn. Curious, Moses stepped closer. Then a voice addressed him from within the bush and identified itself as the God of his forefathers: 'I am the God of your father, the God of Abraham, the God of Isaac and the God of Jacob' (Exod. 3:6). In a very direct conversation, Moses then learned what that God called him to do – to liberate his people from their misery in Egypt.

At that point, one can ask whether Moses, the fatherless son, even knew the God of his fathers and what connected him with 'his' people. We can understand him well when he said to God, 'Who am I to go to Pharaoh and bring the Israelites out of Egypt?' (Exod. 3:11). Who was he indeed? And what legitimacy did he have before the Israelites for that mission? When he told them the God of their fathers had sent him, they would want to know who that God was and his name.

And here it came – the turning of God. This was not the God of the past, of the patriarchs, who now gave the order, but the one of the future who proclaims the I Am. 'I am the I Am' (Exod. 3:14). God bears the I-name, the name human beings should also be able to call themselves. It was for this that Moses had to leave Egypt. He had to overcome the Egyptian in him, whom he had outwardly slain forty years earlier. The era of ego development was then dawning in heaven and on Earth, and it would find its completion in the coming of Christ.

Moses became God's agent, through whom the people of Israel initially became aware of a new soul force. A radical change of consciousness had taken its first tentative steps. In the lecture he gave on March 9, 1911, Rudolf Steiner said that the cosmic spirit Moses was ordained to apprehend was of a very different character:

> Its revelation can alone take place in the innermost and holiest midpoint of soul life, the ego. There works the spirit of the universe – in the place where the human soul is conscious of its very centre.[3]

God's self-revelation went hand in hand with a new human quality, one that would still need many centuries of development before it could be fulfilled by Christ. The witness who would finally bring the mission to completion was Paul. In his Epistle to the Galatians, he formulated the fulfilment of his own soul's centre through Christ in his famous phrase, 'But I live; yet now not I, but Christ lives in me' (Gal. 2:20).

This 'I', which is both personal and separate and yet at the same time a reflection of the universal divine 'I' itself, appeared for the first time in the encounter between Moses and God. This became astonishingly clear in the conversation between the two when Moses more or less refused his mission. He doubted whether his people would acknowledge him as God's agent, and he pointed out that he lacked the gift of speech. 'Send anyone else but not me,' he said. And yet perhaps it was just this that demonstrated Moses' suitability for the task. In his refusal, his opposition, something germinated that would come to fruition in the future: the gradual assertion of independence. In Moses, the I Am had found a first herald of humanity, one who, significantly, became so almost against his will.

6. Moses Does Not Enter the Promised Land

Humans continually thirst. In the Old and New Testaments, situations involving thirsty individuals are often those of testing, revealing the nature of those who meet at the well or spring. At the well, God reveals himself and is recognised (although sometimes not). Thus, Christ reveals himself to the Samaritan woman at Jacob's well, and she recognises him. Thirst is an excellent opportunity for knowledge of God.

~

After the exodus from Egypt and the journey through the desert, thirst was a constant test for the Israelites. If they had stayed in Egypt, they could have lived in slavery but without hunger and thirst. They would have been spared much, such as Pharaoh and his army's life-threatening persecution right at the beginning of their journey. But God averted that danger. The army of the Egyptians drowned in the Sea of Reeds after the Israelites had crossed safely. Moses and the people then sang a song of praise.

After just three days in the desert, the thirst came. Only a moment ago, the people had been grateful for their salvation; now they were grumbling against Moses because they couldn't find water. And when they did find some, it was bitter and undrinkable.

Moses turned to God and found out what to do: 'the Lord showed him a piece of wood; he threw it into the water, and it became sweet' (Exod. 15:25). But still the people grumbled. They would rather have died in Egypt, where they sat around pots of meat and had bread in abundance, than to have suffered hardship and deprivation in the desert for the sake of a vague promise. Nevertheless, they always got what they needed, whether it was bread from heaven or water from a rock. The next water miracle happened at Rephidim when the people complained of thirst and wished to return to Egypt. At God's command, Moses struck a rock with his staff, the same staff with which he had made the Nile water undrinkable for the Egyptians. Immediately water gushed out of the rock and the people were able to drink (Exod. 17:5–6).

Every further hardship became a new test for Israel, which it passed with less success than the previous one. After all, experience should have taught them that they would always have enough.

Although Moses had to endure much from these people, he remained faithful to them. He was as faithful as God, who from the burning bush had entrusted him with the tremendous task of the exodus and the journey through the desert. He was the most faithful mediator, entirely in service to the task of leading the people of Israel into the promised land.

Moses, despite his anger, interceded for his people before God after they had danced around the golden calf (Exod. 32). He interceded for his sister, Miriam, when she questioned his authority and mediation and was therefore punished with leprosy (Num. 12). And Moses prevented God from destroying his people when the scouts sent out to the promised land of Canaan reported back and the people were in uproar at what they heard, saying it would have been better if they had stayed in Egypt rather than risk taking on the fearsomely strong Canaanites (Num. 13). Moses,

6. MOSES DOES NOT ENTER THE PROMISED LAND

as well as his brother, Aaron, suffered from the Israelites' lack of trust. The Israelites wanted to stone them after being exposed to such hardship and danger (Num. 14:10). Yet Moses asked God to forgive these people, and through his intercession God forgave them.

In the end, God's faithfulness to his chosen people took on a different aspect to that which had still existed after the people idolised the golden calf. He did not abandon his people, but the present generation would not enter the promised land. Only a faithful few would reach the destination; all the others died during the years of wandering in the wilderness. Those were forty long years, years of probation and of tests not really passed. But those years were time enough for a new generation to grow up, one that had not even been born when the exodus from Egypt took place. That seemed to be the only way. The old were too attached to the past to be ready for what was coming.

Thus, the forty years in the desert was less a period of probation – for that failed – than a time of renewal. Emil Bock calls it a 'time of dying away'.[1] The Egyptian past had to be radically stripped away; the desert generation had to die. That was what their experience taught them on the long path to the land where Christ would come to Earth many centuries later. It was the path of the development of the self, which in many respects is a most difficult birth. Bock formulates this very beautifully:

> Only the younger generation, in which the magnetic recollection of the world of Egypt no longer stood in the way of the budding 'I' impulse and which, from birth, had instead absorbed the landscape of homelessness and egohood, was in a position to enter the land by the Jordan.[2]

Nevertheless, it is extraordinary that the man who had expended all his strength and perseverance, and whose confidence was steeled by the struggles of others and by God's constant help, did not enter the land beyond the Jordan. Moses did not enter the promised land; it was only shown to him from the summit of Mount Nebo. When the 'servant of the Lord' died he was a hundred and twenty years old. 'And no one has known his grave until this day' (Deut. 34). Why was his greatness in vain?

~

Again, the people thirsted. This time it was in Kadesh, where Miriam had just died, towards the end of their forty-year journey in the wilderness. The people quarreled with Moses and Aaron. It was a situation very similar to the beginning in Rephidim. Nothing seemed to have changed. God, however, spoke to Moses a little differently.

> Take the staff, and you and your brother Aaron gather the assembly together. Speak to that rock before their eyes, and it will pour out its water. You will bring water out of the rock for the community so they and their livestock can drink.

So Moses took the staff from the Lord's presence, just as he commanded him. He and Aaron gathered the assembly together in front of the rock, and Moses said to them, 'Listen, you rebels, must we bring you water out of this rock?' Then Moses raised his arm and struck the rock twice with his staff. Water gushed out, and the community and their livestock drank.

But then the Lord said to Moses and Aaron:

> Because you did not trust in me enough to honor me as holy in the sight of the Israelites, you will not bring this

community into the land I give them. (Num. 20:8–12)

Shortly before the goal, Moses, who had always been so faithful, was rejected. That was a hard blow. What had he done wrong?

It is difficult to say. There are only a few differences to the situation in Rephidim where Moses also struck the rock with his staff. God now commanded him to take the staff and gather the community together with his brother. But then came a new 'how' of giving water – namely, with the word: 'Speak to that rock before their eyes, and it will pour out its water. You will bring water out of the rock for the community so they and their livestock can drink.'

But the situation was too similar to the one in Rephidim, at the beginning of the wilderness wanderings, for Moses not to fall into its pattern. The staff was his special sign: he had performed miracles with it, and it constituted his authority. Even now, he struck the rock with it, twice this time, and said to the people, 'Listen, you rebels, must we bring you water out of this rock?' Moses blustered. He made the people's behaviour ('you rebels') a reference to himself, and the fact that he repeated the earlier situation with emphasis (striking twice) gave his actions the air of a power that seemed to be entirely his own. Moses assumed an authority in which he did not give glory to God but instead took the renewed water miracle as credit to himself. In striking the rock, when he had been instructed to *speak* to it before the eyes of the people, his attention was diverted from the word to his own power.

Certainly, this is a strong interpretation of what is only weakly expressed in the events. Is it exaggerated? We do not easily come to terms with this biblical passage because something so small had such great consequences. Moses was denied his goal.

Moses was a man of transition, a forerunner of the new who nevertheless remained attached to the old. He was on his way towards the reality of the Christ-imbued 'I' as Saint Paul was to experience it later, but that path was infinitely long. Moses brought the law, not grace. That was his 'fault', which nevertheless cannot be attributed to him – for how could he have understood all that was to come? The law remained, but it was not enough. Moses failed tragically, which was what makes him so outstanding. He was the first to whom the I Am, the World-I, revealed itself. He was on his way from the old to the new but was unable to reach it.

Emil Bock creates a beautiful explanation by making Moses' tragedy understandable through the parallel with John the Baptist. With their own fate, they had 'to seal the destiny of a turning point in time'.[3] They both stood at a threshold without crossing over, but that did not diminish their importance. On the contrary, it had the greatness of a sacrificial act, remaining behind for the sake of others, for the goal of humanity. But Moses, like John, had one distinction – a knowledge of God that no one else had: 'The Lord spoke to Moses face to face, as a man speaks to his friend' (Exod. 33:11).

7. Rahab: Preparing the Way

For forty years, Moses had led the people of Israel through the desert to reach the promised land beyond the Jordan, but he himself could not enter it. With Moses, who paved the way, the old died out, just as during the desert wanderings the old generation also died away. They were replaced by younger people who hardly remembered Egypt or who were born in the desert. Moses was replaced by Joshua, authorised by Moses and by God himself. Under Moses, Joshua was one of the scouts sent to Canaan, most of whom, considered the conquest of the land impossible. Joshua saw things differently and sought to encourage the people. For this, he was almost stoned to death (Num. 14).

Joshua was one of the great trusting ones who nevertheless had to struggle again and again with his fear. In that uncertainty, he experienced divine strengthening and, finally, the instruction, 'Now then, you and all these people, get ready to cross the Jordan River into the land I am about to give to them – to the Israelites' (Josh. 1:2).

Before crossing the threshold of the Jordan, Joshua sent two scouts to the city of Jericho because it was the first to be taken when the land was conquered. According to the biblical account, however, it appeared to be an impregnable fortress with its mighty walls and tightly locked gates. The people in the city were vigilant against threats from outside. It therefore did not go unnoticed that strangers, namely Joshua's scouts, had entered the 'house of a prostitute'. As a public house, it may have suggested itself to the scouts as a place where they would go unnoticed. But they were immediately recognised, and Jericho's king sent a message to Rahab, the prostitute, to hand over the Israelites.

Rahab is one of the very special women in the Bible, whose dazzling independence is a source of wonder. She is one of four significant women in the Old Testament who pave the way for Jesus and thus for the physical basis of the incarnation of Christ. Along with Tamar, Ruth and Bathsheba, she is one of the 'mothers of God' named in Matthew's genealogy of Jesus (Matt. 1:5). Her name can be derived from its Hebrew root, *rachab*, that is, 'to make wide, to open' or 'wide, broad, open'. In that sense, it can be interpreted symbolically as the opening of that closed city or the opening of the 'womb' from which Boaz, one of the progenitors of Jesus, would eventually emerge. To be able to take on that very task, Rahab must not be allowed to perish with Israel during the conquest of the land, which began with the destruction of Jericho. Otherwise, that family tree would not have come into being. Is that coincidence or providence?

Rahab did not hand over the two scouts but let them go unmolested. The scouts were therefore able to report to the people of Israel and prepare them for the capture of the city. Rahab made that possible. She hid Joshua's men under drying flax stalks on the roof of her house and pointed her city's royal messengers in the wrong direction.

> Yes, the men came to me, but I did not know where they
> had come from. At dusk, when it was time to close the city

7. RAHAB: PREPARING THE WAY

gate, they left. I don't know which way they went. Go after them quickly. You may catch up with them. (Josh. 2:4–5)

Why did Rahab do that? She led her people astray and thus betrayed her hometown to the strangers who would destroy it. For Paul in Hebrews, that seemed clear: 'By faith, the prostitute Rahab, because she welcomed the spies, was not killed with those who were disobedient' (Heb. 11:31). But is Paul's interpretation satisfactory?

Rahab, together with her parents and siblings, survived the destruction of Jericho.[1] She allowed the two scouts to escape over the city wall with the help of a rope and, in return, extracted an oath from the two men to spare her house during the conquest. They agreed that she should tie a red rope to her window as a sign to the conquerors that they were to leave that house untouched. The colour of the rope was reminiscent of the sacrificial lamb's blood the Israelites daubed on their doorframes during the Passover night in Egypt to spare their first-born sons from the angel of death. The first-born sons of the Egyptians, however, were killed, which finally persuaded Pharaoh to let the Israelites go (Exod. 12). Thus, the exodus from Egypt and the entry into the land of Canaan were directly related to each other, as was the safe passage through the Sea of Reeds and the impending crossing of the Jordan (Josh. 3:16).

Rahab stood as an enabler at a central point in this story. She knew the intentions of the Israelites and their history:

> I know that the Lord has given you this land and that a great fear of you has fallen on us so that all who live in this country are melting in fear because of you. We have heard how the Lord dried up the water of the Sea of Reeds for

you when you came out of Egypt and what you did to
Sihon and Og, the two kings of the Amorites east of the
Jordan, whom you completely destroyed. When we heard
of it, our hearts sank and everyone's courage failed because
of you. (Josh. 2:9–11)

News of what the people of Israel had achieved with the help of their God struck fear into the hearts of the land's inhabitants.

What were Rahab's motives in her encounter with the emissaries of that powerful foreign people, which led to her betraying her city? Two possibilities suggest themselves. First, Rahab was also afraid of the foreigners and saw an opportunity to save herself and her relatives through an alliance with the 'enemy'. As a psychological interpretation this does not necessarily speak in Rahab's favour.

The second possibility is that Rahab – as Saint Paul thinks – recognised the 'true' God when she said, 'for the Lord your God is God above in heaven and below on Earth', and that she sensed the Mother-God mystery and perceived a mission of destiny. Was she in contact with the world spirit to whom she was here knowingly offering her hand to fulfil what was necessary? Or was God using her for his purposes?

Both the psychological and the salvation-plan interpretations leave one unsatisfied. One is all too human, whereas the other bears the problem of an instrumental understanding of history in which things seem to be pre-arranged.

It is not easy to discern a third possibility, and yet the personality of this woman, who is neither cowardly nor calculating, demands one. Rahab worked out of her independence. Unlike hardly any other person in this narrative, Rahab worked out of her own individual, independent nature. This is evident from the fact that, apart from Joshua, she is the only one mentioned by name. She

7. RAHAB: PREPARING THE WAY

stood alone and for herself, in contrast to the scouts, the king of Jericho, and his messengers. She acted quickly and decisively, and in her knowledge and actions she appeared sovereign rather than fearful. She did what the situation demanded without giving the impression that she was forced to do anything. She confessed that the country's inhabitants had succumbed to a paralysing terror, but she was anything but paralysed as she hid the two men that the royal messengers ordered her to hand over; and she professed her allegiance to the God of Israel when she asked the men to swear to her 'by the Lord' to show mercy to her and her father's house as she did to them (Josh. 2:12).

Rahab was a woman who lived outside the norms of society. For the people of Israel, she was the stranger who, however, became an extraordinary confessor of Yahweh. She is probably most similar to the Samaritan woman in the New Testament whom Christ met at the well and who, with her six husbands, her non-Jewish origin, and unconventional way of acting, had a similarly 'subversive' effect.[2] In her entire appearance, Rahab undermined a clear sorting according to good and evil, right and wrong.

Both women encountered something new with Yahweh and the Messiah. It was an encounter that was not to be expected. Strangers came to Rahab's house, and the Samaritan woman spoke to a strange man at the well. Rahab is called a 'prostitute' in the text, but the narrative does not seem to take offence at her trade. In any case, it marked her as an unmarried and independent woman who may have had to support herself through prostitution. Since the time of the Church Father Justin Martyr, the Christian point of view has often retrospectively understood her to be a woman who converted to the true faith from her 'sinfulness' as a whore. But that is not how she appeared. Rahab did not allow herself to be used as an instrument. Rather, as her name suggests, she appeared open to what was to come and left behind the old. At the same time, being a foreigner (similar to Ruth, the Moabitess, later on), Israel received a new, outside element through her. The story undermined the 'purity' of the lineage, weaving it together with something new. Israel's people had continuously yearned for Egypt during their wanderings. Through Rahab, the exodus was finally accomplished.

8. Samson: God-sent Yet Independent

Between the conquest of the promised land and the establishment of the state of Israel, the people of Israel were accompanied by a succession of twelve leaders whom the Old Testament calls judges. The last of those twelve worthy leaders was Samson. A hero who, in modern terms, was also an anti-hero. He was an adventurer, the one with the powers of Heracles, the one who conquered and failed. Like Moses and John the Baptist, Samson too was denied the ultimate fulfilment for all his efforts. His remarkable victory over the Philistines, who would only truly be overcome by King David, cost Samson his life. He was a man of extraordinary physical strength, strong desires and great weaknesses. All of this was most evident on a personal level. Nevertheless, his deeds and his person have something charismatic about them and are an integral part of God's history with his people Israel.

For all his ambivalence, Samson was consecrated to God from the beginning. Like Isaac and later John the Baptist, whose parents also had no hope of having children, he was the child of an infertile woman. But the angel of the Lord appeared and said:

> You are barren and childless, but you are going to become pregnant and give birth to a son. Now see to it that you

drink no wine or other fermented drink and that you do not eat anything unclean. You will become pregnant and have a son whose head is never to be touched by a razor because the boy is to be a Nazirite, dedicated to God from the womb. He will take the lead in delivering Israel from the hands of the Philistines. (Judg. 13:3–5)

The angel gave the expectant mother the provisions that belong to the Nazirite vow, as Moses had already laid them down (Num. 6) and would, in the end, be fulfilled by John the Baptist. According to the Hebrew 'nazir', Nazirite means 'consecrated', 'set apart'. A Nazirite was supposed to keep away from wine and other intoxicating drinks and, in general, from everything that came from the vine. He was to avoid everything animal, so he was a vegetarian in the strictest sense. He was not allowed to go near a dead person. In addition, he was in contact with God's solar power through his hair, which was why it was not allowed to be cut. The fact that abstinence from wine and 'unclean' food was already imposed on Samson's mother expressed that his consecration was not Samson's decision but came from God. Samson was destined for divine service.

But while John the Baptist would observe these regulations, Samson broke with every single one. This does not mean that he resisted his commission. Rather, we encounter in Samson an enormous tension between self-empowerment and the fulfilment of his mission, between self-determination and predestination. The peculiar thing is that Samson's nature did not make him a consecrated man, yet he did not rebel against the consecration imposed upon him. He fulfilled it in all his wildness. He was an explosive adventurer who did not fit at all into the image of a leader of his people but was nevertheless completely in the service of Yahweh. That is the charm of his story.

8. SAMSON: GOD-SENT YET INDEPENDENT

Samson's wilfulness is immediately apparent to us in the first episode we read about him. As a grown man, Samson went down to the city of Timnah where he saw a young woman he decided he wanted to marry. The fact that the woman was a Philistine of all things, and his parents objected to the marriage, did not bother him. It had to be that woman. As Samson passed through vineyards (which he was supposed to avoid) on his way to the courtship, a young, roaring lion came rushing towards him. He tore the lion apart 'as he might have torn a young goat' (Judg. 14:6), demonstrating his strength for the first time. Shortly afterwards, Samson met with his bride-to-be and talked with her.

A few days later, as he was going down to marry the young woman, Samson turned from his path to check on the carcass of the lion. This was against the Nazirite rules to stay away from animals and anything dead. Samson found a swarm of bees in the body of the dead lion and honey upon which he fed.

This episode set the stage for Samson's first battle with the Philistines. It occurred during his wedding when he gave the thirty companions at the feast a riddle based on his encounter with the lion, something that was impossible for them to guess. If they solved it, he told them, he would give each one a linen garment and a set of clothes. The riddle was, 'Out of the eater, something to eat; out of the strong, something sweet.' Samson could be certain of his victory, but his bride wrested the secret from him. Pressed by her fellow tribesmen she demanded Samson prove his love for her by telling her the answer, which she then passed onto her people. They then gave Samson the solution as a new riddle: 'What is sweeter than honey? What is stronger than a lion?' (Judg. 14:18). Samson realised he had been betrayed by his bride, the one person above all others who should have been faithful to him. Out of revenge, Samson went down to Ashkelon where he killed thirty Philistines, stripped them of their clothes and gave them to the thirty companions who had explained his riddle. He honoured his wager but did so in the most brutal manner.

Since he had entrusted his bride with the secret to prove his love, their new riddle emerged from it. What is it that is sweeter than honey and stronger than the lion? It is love. And it was just this love that his bride betrayed. In his anger, the spirit of God came upon Samson, which served only to incite it further. This is a curious feature of Samson's story: the actions that proceed from his wild nature nevertheless align with God's plan. For the fact that his eye fell on a Philistine woman in the first place was entirely in accordance with the divine purpose. Samson's parents objected because they did not know 'that this was from the Lord, who was seeking an occasion to confront the Philistines' (Judg. 14:4). It was just such an opportunity that the Philistines would offer Samson again and again. He never initiated the attacks, but always responded to their attacks.

Samson had an intimate relationship with the Philistines, especially through his three love affairs with Philistine women. Thus, he would fight the Philistines from within. When his first anger was spent, he wanted to go to his wife. It turned out that in the meantime, her father had married her off to someone else. Her father then offered Samson her sister, which must have seemed like a mockery to Samson, so he took revenge again. He destroyed the Philistines' entire harvest with three hundred foxes to whose tails he tied burning torches, chasing them into the fields. In turn, the Philistines took revenge on the woman's family, even as they pursued Samson.

When Samson fell into Philistine hands, the 'spirit of the Lord' came upon him again, and he freed himself. He found a fresh donkey's jawbone (again something dead) and slew a thousand

8. SAMSON: GOD-SENT YET INDEPENDENT

Philistines with it. After that, there was a long period of peace because it says, 'Samson led (judged) Israel for twenty years in the days of the Philistines' (Judg. 15:20).

But then there were renewed acts of strength. The next one was again related to a woman. Samson visited a Philistine prostitute in Gaza. The townspeople surrounded the house to ambush and kill him, but Samson escaped at midnight. He seized the doors of the city gate, lifted them onto his shoulders, and carried them up Mount Hebron as proof of his extraordinary strength. Who could take on such a man?

'Some time later,' it says succinctly, 'he fell in love with a woman in the Valley of Sorek whose name was Delilah' (Judg. 16:4). Once more Samson came into contact with the vine, for Sorek is the 'valley of grapes'. The lords of the Philistines now offered Delilah a large bribe in silver pieces to extract the secret of Samson's power. Delilah made three attempts to uncover his secret and three times she was deceived by Samson. Then she followed the same pattern as Samson's bride and demanded proof of love: 'How can you say, "I love you," when you won't confide in me?' Every day she prodded him in this way until he became 'sick to death' of it. Then he told her everything and revealed that the secret of his strength lay in his hair (Judg. 16:16–17).

Samson, once strong and unassailable, had made himself vulnerable. At the same time, he had betrayed his mission, because he revealed the secret of his special relationship with God. That betrayal was his weakness, and he became weak through the betrayal. His hair was shorn, which meant no less than 'that the Lord had departed from him.' Just as God gave his people into their enemies' hands when they fell away from him, so now Samson also fell completely into Philistine hands. They gouged out his eyes and set him to hard labour.

Samson's story reflects what was generally true of the Old Testament Book of Judges. In the land given to it, Israel was not free in two respects. On the one hand the land was still inhabited and Israel was threatened outwardly by other peoples; on the other, Israel was inwardly unfree because it repeatedly fell into idolatry. God punished their turning away from him by giving them into the hands of their enemies. But when they cried out for help, God gave them a judge who sought to free them again, which went hand in hand with their renewed faithfulness to God.

Samson became that judge. He found his way back to Yahweh in a powerful manner by deciding his own death sentence.

The Philistines celebrated the defeat of the strong man with a feast of thanksgiving to their god Dagon. Overconfident, the Philistines led in the now blinded Samson to entertain the revelers. He asked the servant who was leading him to put him next to the pillars that supported the temple so that he might lean against them. Three thousand men and women were gathered in that temple, rejoicing over their conquered enemy. But Samson, whose hair had meanwhile grown back, pushed against the pillars with all his strength, toppling them and collapsing the temple. In doing so, he took all those inside with him to their deaths: 'Thus he killed many more when he died than while he lived' (Judg. 16:30). The Philistines' hour of greatest triumph became the hour of their defeat. It was the beginning of the end for them. What had to happen, happened.

As a devotee of God, Samson was completely at the service of liberation. Though he seems to have behaved so capriciously, he fulfilled his mission – even though he transgressed all the Nazirite commandments and seemed to follow only his own interests. This is the most amazing thing about his story. What does this mean? In the worst case, it could mean that it doesn't matter what a person

8. SAMSON: GOD-SENT YET INDEPENDENT

does because God uses everything for his purposes. But that is not how the relationship between humans and God appears in the Samson story.

From a modern perspective, we can see in Samson an illustration of the central problem that lies in the tension between individual freedom and divine predestination. Samson was predestined to be a devotee of God but repeatedly did things incompatible with this. Was he therefore one who rebelled? No, Samson was not an Old Testament Prometheus. Nevertheless, there was in him a budding ego power that pointed to the future.

From birth, Samson was aligned with his mission, even if he deviated from it and had to drastically experience his weakness. That his strength was part of his nature was proven when his hair grew back and he thus regained his power. But that alone was not enough. Added to this was his faithfulness to God, which he found above all in physical need. Physical need was the reason why Samson prayed. That happened twice. The first time was after he had slain a thousand Philistines with the donkey's jawbone. Afterwards, he thirsted and said to God, 'You have given your servant this great victory. Must I now die of thirst and fall into the hands of the uncircumcised?' (Judg. 15:18). Then God split a rock and let water flow out of it. Samson drank and was revived.

At the Philistines' celebratory feast, where Samson appeared defeated and humiliated, he prayed a second time: 'Sovereign Lord, remember me. Please, God, strengthen me just once more, and let me with one blow get revenge on the Philistines for my two eyes' (Judg. 16:28). Certainly, that prayer was under the sign of revenge, but at the same time there was a conscious reference to God. Samson knew that he owed his strength to God, and once again he wanted to work out of this. In his death, his self-willed action coincided with the mission that had been given to him from birth.

He did not resist what had been imposed upon him, yet he expressed his own will through it.

Samson remains a dazzling figure, which does not prevent us from seeing references to Christ in his story. The announcement of Samson's birth can be compared with that of Jesus. Samson was consecrated to God and driven by the Lord who came upon him. He thirsted in the throes of death and was betrayed for pieces of silver. He cried out to God and was heard, and he performed his greatest act of deliverance in his death – all these are references to Christ. Though distant from Christ in some ways, Samson was also close to him in others. Between Samson and Christ lie the metamorphoses of a mighty history. Samson's name, which means 'little sun', testifies to their closeness to each other.

9. Ruth: The Stranger in Jesus' Family Tree

She was a quiet and devotedly acquiescent woman who yet had a strong will. She seems to have had a goal in mind without being able to name it. In any case, she was defined by a certainty about life that convinced those around her and also us as readers. And she played a role in the history of Israel, for she would become the great-grandmother of King David and thus enters the ancestral line of Jesus – Ruth, the Moabitess, the stranger in Israel, who foreshadows the collapse of the borders between peoples (see the Book of Ruth and Matthew 1:5).

Ruth's mission to become a link in the chain of a foreign people – a chain that would lead to a new religion – magnetically attracted all her actions. She acted with impressive single-mindedness when she couldn't know where it would all lead. Everything fell into place, and yet, with Ruth, a single individual was actively involved. Perhaps that is the epitome of trust in God. But Ruth's mother-in-law, Naomi, the other main character in this story, also acted in a powerful way, despite her apparent powerlessness as a childless widow in a foreign land. Naomi's husband and her two sons had died, but in the end she was fortunate enough to have a grandson born to her. A 'redeemer' guaranteed Naomi the continuation of her clan and, ultimately, paved the way for

Christ's incarnation over a thousand years later. How did that come about?

A famine in Bethlehem caused Elimelek to move with his wife Naomi and his two sons, Mahlon ('the sickly one') and Kilion ('the weak one'), to the East Jordanian land of the Moabites. He sought his future in that quiet and carefree region (see Jeremiah 48:11). Elimelek has been seen as an apostate who left Israel's promised land and did not trust in his God in times of trouble. His emigration did not profit him, for he died, and with him his two sons, whose names already hint at their missing future. Both the sickly and the weak had married Moabite women but remained childless. After the deaths of the men, it was the women's turn.

As a widow and a foreigner, Naomi was doubly defenceless in a foreign land. When she learned that the famine in her homeland was over, she returned to the land of Judah. Her daughters-in-law accompanied her at first, but then Naomi asked them to return 'each to her mother's house'. She herself could not give them new husbands, but in their Moabite homeland there was a good chance of remarriage.

Over the years, an intimate relationship must have grown, for Orpah and Ruth, the two daughters-in-law, wept and said, 'We want to go with you to your people.' Orpah ('the turning away') eventually returned to her parental home, while Ruth ('the friend') insisted on moving to her mother-in-law's homeland, even though she could expect rejection there. Her words expressed her strong will:

> Do not urge me to leave you or to turn back from you.
> Where you go, I will go, and where you stay, I will stay.
> Your people will be my people, and your God my God.
> Where you die, I will die, and there I will be buried.

9. RUTH: THE STRANGER IN JESUS' FAMILY TREE

May the Lord deal with me, be it ever so severely, if even death separates you and me. (Ruth 1:16–17)

She even confirms her decision with an oath of imprecation, calling on God to punish her if she did not keep her word.

Unlike her father-in-law, Elimelek, she did not leave her own country for the selfish reasons of a better life but rather chose an uncertain future with privations. Elimelek thought he was escaping death in his homeland, but he ran straight to it in a foreign land. Elimelek's name, 'God is king', subtly hints at this thwarting of his intentions. It is God who determines. And yet humans also act. Ruth, usually translated as 'friend', 'companion', or 'neighbour', is the complementary counter-image to Elimelek. She walked into uncertainty but would still win life. One is reminded of Matthew 16:25: 'For whoever wants to save his life will lose it, but whoever loses his life for me will find it.' Ruth, who seems to fit completely into her mother-in-law's story and thus into Israel's, nevertheless did so in all self-determination, for she resisted Naomi's well-intentioned invitation to leave her. In a foreign country, she would seek paths to her own and her mother-in-law's salvation with a persistent acquiescence that seems so determined by faith, love and hope, that it also affects those around her.

Ruth knew how to bring about harmony with the world as a whole. She had a radiance that was granted success. Perhaps in her, we encounter an anticipation of a soul capacity, which only an individual who stands on their own can unfold. As a stranger far away from her homeland, she gained an independence that seemed to contradict the primacy of family and clan. And yet she would help her mother-in-law, who lived by that maxim, to have and preserve the offspring she longed for.

Ruth started her life in a foreign land on a small scale. As a gleaner, she made use of the law that allowed the poor to gather small amounts of grain left behind after the harvest. She had to work hard in Bethlehem's fields to earn what the fields of Moab had granted her father-in-law without difficulty. But she chose the right place, namely the fields belonging to Boaz, a widely respected man whose name means 'the strong one', in contrast to the significant names of Naomi's sons – the sickly and the weak ones.

This strong man, however, was as tender as he was resolute. He seems like Ruth's father, for he addressed her with a 'Do you hear me, my daughter?' He had watched her and was impressed. A servant who had been overseeing the harvest brought him an almost commanding request from her: 'Please let me glean and gather among the sheaves behind the harvesters.' (Ruth 2:7). This 'let me...', repeated in her speeches, reflected her nature. She wanted only a small thing, but she wanted it with a determination that is capable of making it great. Ruth wanted to feed herself and her mother-in-law. She wanted nothing given as her father-in-law had once given, but only to pick up the crumbs that fall from the table of the great. And, as Boaz's servant reported, she 'has come and stayed there from the morning until now and has rested but little.' This foreign woman's faithfulness and endurance impressed the strong man. He placed her under his protection and favoured her in every way.

Naomi, on her arrival in Bethlehem, renamed herself Mara, meaning 'the bitter', because she saw herself struck by misfortune. From there, however, she was able to find her way back to her essence, as expressed by her original name, 'the lovely'. In Boaz's actions, she saw a sign that God had not turned away from her and her dead after all. For Boaz was one of her deceased husband's kin, which meant he could be a 'redeemer'. That is, he belonged to the

9. RUTH: THE STRANGER IN JESUS' FAMILY TREE

circle of those relatives who were obliged to rescue relatives from distress and ensure the preservation of the male offspring entitled to inherit from men who had died childless. The first son born in such an 'in-law marriage' was considered a descendant of the deceased.

Naomi then recognised the double opportunity to see Ruth provided for in the future and also to gain a clan-sustaining grandson. She asked Ruth to take a daring step: she should bathe, anoint herself, put on a dress, and then lie down at Boaz's feet on the threshing floor where he would sleep at night after the harvest. That step was as unconventional as the one taken by Tamar, Judah's daughter-in-law, who, twice widowed and childless, disguised herself as a prostitute to seduce her father-in-law in order to procreate with him. The result had been Perez, a forefather of Boaz.

Things are more 'decent' here, however. They happen in a more orderly manner. Boaz did not allow himself to be seduced for there was another relative, one more closely related, who had a right and thus a duty towards Ruth and her deceased husband. But this other relative did not want to fulfill their duty because his first-born son would then legally be the heir of another. Here it becomes clear that the actions of Boaz, who would marry Ruth, also had something of a sacrifice about them, for he renounced the chance of having his first-born be his own son and heir.

To us, however, it is in just this renunciation that he appears to live out a dignity that pays appropriate tribute to the nature of his future wife. Both the already older man and the young widow, the strong man and the young woman, are equals. This quality of the relationship leaves us as readers with a good sense of coherence. Everything fell into place as it should, neither of the main characters appear to us to be forced or unfree. Naomi finally held her grandson Obed, whose name means 'the servant'. This shows that everyone had reached their goal, contributing their share, and that everything happened in the gesture of service. Serving does not mean giving up one's own interests but rather acquiring them in serving. The idea of the clan underwent an expansion that would only be fulfilled in the true sense in Christian times. The barriers between peoples would fall and the 'foreigner', the 'outsider', was part of it. Naomi was written into that expansion through a grandson who was in no way genetically related to her.

The Book of Ruth is a piece of literature, a composition. The revealing names of the characters testify to this. Yet the story is not fiction. It has its place in the great history of humankind, which always has surprises in store. Who would have thought that a famine in Bethlehem would have anything to do with the birth of Jesus over a thousand years later?

10. Saul and the Necromancer: A King's End

Saul was the first king of Israel, the defender and upholder of God's laws. Among them was the following: 'You shall not turn to the necromancers of spirits and the interpreters of signs, nor consult them, lest you become unclean in them' (Lev. 19:31). For Saul to break that law would be considered sacrilege, but that is just what he did when faced with a renewed and particularly threatening Philistine deployment. How would that battle turn out? What was in store for him?

Saul was already in a volatile state due to his past history. That history included military successes but all too many shadows, including a psyche prone to gloom, jealousy of his brilliant successor, David, and, above all, condemnations by God. Twice he had acted against God's commandments. The first time was when, before a battle against the Philistines, he did not want to wait for the prophet Samuel to bring the burnt offering to propitiate God. Saul, who was not authorised to do so, brought it himself, probably because the people threatened to run away from him if he did not take action as the Philistines drew closer (1Sam. 13:8–9).

After he had brought the sacrifice, Samuel appeared and rebuked him sharply. He announced that Saul's kingship would not last because he had not obeyed God's command. At the same time, he gave him to understand that God had chosen someone else 'after his own heart'. 'Already?' one thinks here because the shepherd David was meant. Samuel would anoint him at God's command a little later, solely in the presence of his brothers, thus almost in secret (1Sam. 16:13).

The second time Saul was guilty before God was in connection with his victorious campaign against the Amalekites. Here Saul only captured the enemy king and carried away the enemy's best animals to sacrifice them later. According to God's instructions, however, he should have completed his command to destroy the king and everything belonging to him. That is, he should have completely destroyed the enemy of Israel. From Samuel, Saul now had to be told harshly, 'Obedience is better than sacrifice', and 'Because you have rejected the word of the Lord, he has also rejected you, that you should no longer be king' (1Sam. 15:22–23). Thus, Saul was king only provisionally. When David entered Saul's service, he had already been appointed his successor.

David was God's favourite who succeeded in everything, such as the battle against the Philistine giant Goliath. He was a gifted harp player who could soothe Saul's tormented spirit with his music, and he won the friendship of Saul's son Jonathan and the love of his daughter Michal. David was better at everything. It is no wonder that Saul, who had made an honest effort, was jealous. We then see him guilty of attempts to murder David. On the other hand, from a modern point of view, we would not blame him for not waiting for Samuel and for sparing the enemy, with the consequence that he forfeited his kingship.

Saul did not toil under a good star. Again and again, he made mistakes. Although he wanted to do good, he ultimately did not achieve it. In his tragic uncertainty, when he was supposed to act like a king and yet at the same time knew that he no longer was one,

10. SAUL AND THE NECROMANCER

it is understandable that he sought guidance. During his life, the prophet Samuel had always given him wise counsel, but Samuel had since died. Now Saul faced a great battle against the Philistines who threatened to overwhelm him. In the meantime, David had 'fled' to the Philistines to escape Saul's further persecution, although both of them had come closer again. It was a tricky situation in which Saul found himself, and he longed for clarity.

In his distress he first turned to God, but God remained silent. All legitimate means of questioning him – dreams, lottery oracles, prophets – failed. So Saul seized on a last resort. He said to his loyal servant, 'Find me a woman who can summon the dead, that I may go to her and question her' (1Sam. 28:7). In Endor, a place close to the upcoming battle, a woman was found who still practiced that profession. She was, so to speak, 'left over' because Saul had previously driven all the mediums out of the country or even had them 'exterminated' under the law. Incognito and under cover of night, Saul now turned to the very woman who in modern times has often been called the 'witch of Endor'. The woman sensed a trap, for she knew Saul's decree concerning those of her status. When she learned who she was to 'summon up', however, she realised the man who endangered her life stood before her, for no one other than Saul could want her to summon the spirit of Samuel. What danger must Saul have been in to ask such a monstrous thing of her? Perhaps the woman already sensed his great need and therefore did what Saul wanted. She then saw a spirit coming out of the earth, which Saul recognised, according to her description, as Samuel, his ambivalent guide.

Again, the prophet rebuked him sharply, 'Why have you disturbed me by bringing me up?' (1Sam. 28:15). By disturbing the rest of the deceased in Sheol, the world of the dead, Saul had committed the final sacrilege. In despair, Saul explained his great distress to the dead prophet and asked him to tell him what to do. Samuel's answer was merciless and devastating: Saul could do nothing. There were no more possible actions for the king. It was over; his fate was sealed. God would give Saul into the hands of the Philistines because of his transgressions. He would perish. 'Tomorrow you and your sons will be with me' (1Sam. 28:19). The battle with the Philistines would lead Saul and his sons to their deaths. One could hardly imagine such a 'tomorrow'. Saul, who had also fasted beforehand, collapsed, completely debilitated by that sentence. To be so rejected, to be so abandoned by God, although he sought him, was already destruction.

Saul appears here like a kind of Job. But just as Job did everything right in his perceived abandonment of God, Saul did every imaginable wrong. And there is something else different from Job, namely companionship in his misfortune. Job's friends could only see in his misfortune the consequence of a fault they held against him to the end. God interceded for the innocent Job as a witness against his friends.

In Saul's case, the necromancer who had previously been rejected by him on principle, now took pity on Saul. She saw him on the ground and said to him:

> Look, your servant has obeyed you. I took my life in my
> hands and did what you told me to do. Now please listen
> to your servant and let me give you some food so you
> may eat and have the strength to go on your way.
> (1Sam. 28:21–22)

After an initial refusal, Saul obeyed, for mercy is better than sacrifice. He sat down on the bed and the woman prepared an invigorating meal. 'Then she set it before Saul and his men, and

10. SAUL AND THE NECROMANCER

they ate. That same night they got up and left.' (1Sam. 28:25).

The woman of Endor did everything in her power to raise Saul up for his final walk. There was even talk of her slaughtering her fattened calf for him, which was undoubtedly more a symbol of her helpfulness than a realistic action in that situation. This woman was anything but a witch, as she has been repeatedly labelled, especially during witch hunts. It was not a spell of harm that she cast but the spell of deep human solidarity with one who was at his end. It helped him to meet that end with uprightness and dignity. She could not change God's judgment. Nor did Saul attempt to do so. The prophecy given to him by Samuel was not a challenge to him, as the Delphic oracle was to Oedipus, to avoid the fate that had been decreed. He knew that he could only walk towards it.

Saul may not have died a hero's death, but neither did he die unworthily. Badly wounded in the battle against the Philistines, he asked his armour-bearer for the death blow so that those 'uncircumcised' would not make fun of him. But the armour-bearer did not dare. So Saul threw himself on his sword. This death was more an expression of dignity than the shadow of a desperate act of suicide. Saul did not want to be taken alive by the enemy. The last woe that befell him was that his body was dishonoured by the victorious Philistines who displayed it on a city wall. When the inhabitants of the nearby city of Jabesh learned of this, they removed the bodies of Saul and his sons from the wall and gave them an honourable burial.

The encounter between Saul and the woman of Endor was on the highest human level. The king who once towered over all (1Sam. 9:2) was lying on the ground. Then the woman, who it was sacrilegious to visit, turned to him and strengthened him. This did not mean that all the banished soothsayers were now pardoned – that was scarcely possible. But it becomes clear that there was a deeply human, even Christian, compassion towards Saul's misery, granted to one who had fallen so low. Evil generates both deeds and suffering. Saul was not simply someone who had done much wrong. He was also someone who had suffered endlessly because of it, and therefore he deserved mercy.

11. David: Fallible But Forgiven

The name 'David' means 'favourite'. He was Jesse's youngest son and the grandson of Boaz from the tribe of Judah and Ruth, the Moabitess. But he did not seem to be Jesse's favourite in the way that Joseph had been to his father, Jacob. Jesse had almost forgotten his youngest son when it came to finding the one who was to succeed Saul as king. Saul had forfeited his kingship, so much so that God regretted making him king (1Sam. 15:11). Then God wanted to indicate to the prophet Samuel whom he had chosen to succeed Saul. The chosen one would be shown to him at a sacrificial banquet that Samuel was to host in Bethlehem with Jesse and his sons. One son after another passed by Samuel. The first, Eliab, Samuel considered because his tall stature was reminiscent of Saul and had something regal about it. But he was mistaken and had to be told, 'People look at the outward appearance, but the Lord looks at the heart' (1Sam. 16:7). The right heart was one that no one had considered. After the chosen one had not been found among his seven sons, Jesse mentioned his eighth, almost reluctantly, because he was probably out of the question anyway: 'There is still the youngest. He is tending the sheep.' But that would be the one God had chosen, and Samuel received the divine instruction to anoint him.

This was similar to the baptism of Jesus because, 'From that day on the Spirit of the Lord came powerfully upon David.' David, as the anointed one, as a Messiah, becomes the bearer of the spirit. But he led such a changeable and partly guilt-ridden life that one wonders how the spirit could constantly rest on him. His was a life of agitation, kingship, cunning in war, and deep friendship. There was love, sorrow, prayer, desire and failure, gratitude, and self-criticism. Additionally, it was marked by extraordinary musical talent. Yet, at the same time, one can also rejoice that such a life was the epitome of a consecrated life. It demonstrates the whole fullness of what is possible between heaven and Earth.

David was favoured, even if not by his father. He was chosen, divine and human at the same time; he was gifted. But as an anointed one he did not immediately become king. Saul did not cease to be king even though 'the spirit of the Lord' was no longer with him. Indeed, from then on, Saul was frightened by an evil spirit and fell repeatedly into depression. It seems almost ironic that, on the advice of his courtiers, he wanted to treat his condition with music, which David, as an expert string player, would perform for him. David thus came to Saul's court both with his harp and as the anointed one. Every time he played, 'relief would come to Saul; he would feel better, and the evil spirit would leave him' (1Sam. 16:23). The competitor and follower was also the therapist. The relationship between Saul and David, which Saul initially treated like a friendship, was difficult. It almost necessarily turned into enmity and led to years of persecution. But though Saul was angry at David and even wanted to kill him, David did not harbour any hostile feelings towards him. He would sincerely mourn Saul after his death. That was what distinguished him: David never became angry, even though he later incurred guilt at the height of his fame.

11. DAVID: FALLIBLE BUT FORGIVEN

Saul only drew David fully into his court after David's confrontation with Goliath. Saul could not help but honour such a victorious fighter against the ever-threatening Philistines by allowing him to be close. The battle against Goliath was not devoid of comedy – a heavily armed and armoured giant challenged the Israelites to single combat. He seemed invincible, and, as in the fairy tales, the one who defeated him was to be rewarded afterwards with the hand of the king's daughter. David, who protected his sheep from lions and bears, saw no insurmountable difficulty in overcoming this 'uncircumcised one'. Saul dressed David in his own armour, with a brazen helmet, and gave him his royal sword to fight Goliath. But David struggled with it all:

> 'I cannot go in these,' he said to Saul, 'because I am not used to them.' So he took them off. Then he took his staff in his hand, chose five smooth stones from the stream, put them in the pouch of his shepherd's bag, and, with his sling in his hand, approached the Philistine.
> (1Sam. 17:39–40)

As a shepherd with a slingshot, he would overpower the heavily armed giant. He hit him in the forehead with a stone, the giant fell, and David killed him with his own sword.

It was characteristic of the relationship between David and Saul that the future king would not put on the armour of the one still in office. David could not take over Saul's kingship in that way. But immediately after the victory over Goliath, he took on the clothes and armour of Saul's son Jonathan, for they had become intimate friends: 'And Jonathan made a covenant with David because he loved him as himself' (1Sam. 18:3). That covenant also became a covenant against Saul, Jonathan's father, who pursued David even more mercilessly out of jealousy towards the younger and more successful man. David's string playing could no longer free Saul from the evil spirit; instead, Saul's behaviour became increasingly impossible, showing ever more clearly the need for a completely different king.

The new circumstances went against all convention. Jonathan, the king's son, whose clothes David now wore, stood up for his friend against his father. Jonathan, the actual heir to the throne, the one whose inheritance David challenged, loved David 'as himself'. There was a quiet greatness in Jonathan. He demonstrated that greatness towards his father just as David did in a different way towards Goliath. Jonathan was able to acknowledge David's divine election without envy, and to stand behind the anointed one. For that reason, David could put on Jonathan's armour but not Saul's.

Saul persecuted David for years. In his distress, David finally entered into a daring game with the Philistines and allied himself with them against his own people. Saul finally died with Jonathan and three of his other sons in the battle against the Philistines. This finally cleared the way for David's kingship, first over Judah and then, after a few years, the rest of the tribes of Israel including those in the north. The Philistines were driven back and Jerusalem became the capital of David's kingdom as well as its religious center. It was a time of success and splendour, but such times do not last and David soon faced new trials.

At the height of his success, David prepared an abyss into which he then fell. He desired Bathsheba, the wife of Uriah, who was away at war. He asked her to come to his palace. When Bathsheba later became pregnant, David summoned Uriah out of the field and asked him to go home to his wife. Imagining that Uriah would sleep with his wife, David hoped thereby to foist the child onto Uriah. But Uriah remained with his comrades, a decision that would cost him his life. David placed Uriah at the front of the battle, where the fighting was fiercest and where the enemy would inevitably kill him. After the period of mourning was over, Bathsheba officially became David's wife. The king had abused his power and incurred judgment through the double sin of adultery and murder.

But David recognised his guilt and proved to be someone who understood that royal power did not give him the right to act in an arbitrary manner. This was the precondition for God's forgiveness, which did not spare him the punishment. The first son he had with Bathsheba died. The unusual thing about the story, however, is that of all things an adulterous relationship finally produced the heir to David's throne and the forefather of the Jesus born in Matthew's Gospel, for Bathsheba became the mother of Solomon. It was not Michal, the daughter of Saul whom David had legally married, who gave birth to his successor, but rather the wife of another. It is amazing how often human sin becomes a historically powerful component of future meaning. Sin, too, belongs to fulfilment without being justified by it. It confirms the value of freedom. For David, that freedom included self-knowledge: he recognised his guilt and did not seek to repress it.

Another thing about David is that he was free of any need for revenge. He loved, even when he encountered hostility from his beloved. He mourned for his son Absalom as he did for Saul, even though Absalom disputed his kingship. Absalom, David's third son, was extraordinarily beautiful but greedy for power. In the end, David had to flee from his own son as he had once fled from Saul. Only the duplicity of David's friend, who served Absalom as an advisor, made it possible for David's troops to be victorious over those of his son. As a result, David's general Joab killed Absalom. David was overwhelmed by grief at his son's death and he took out his pain and anger on the loyal soldiers who had fought for him. He insulted them until Joab made the reinstated king see reason.

One last time David would be caught in the tension between his personal feelings and his royal duty. Wishing to ascertain his own importance through the number of his followers, he conducted a census. Whoever counts human beings in this way reduces them to a nameless number, and this could only bring disaster. David was aware of this immediately afterwards: 'David was conscience-stricken after he had counted the fighting men' (2Sam. 24:10). However, the punishment for that did not strike him first, but his people – plague broke out. David realised that it had struck the innocent and was prepared to take upon himself the disaster he had caused. Yet that would not be achieved through renewed suffering. Instead, David built an altar at a place designated to him, an altar for atonement and to offer sacrifices of thanksgiving in the future. It was the place where Solomon, his second son with Bathsheba, would build the temple.

12. Job: The Rebellious Sufferer

Job was deprived of everything: his possessions, his children, his health – everything except his life. He was a great sufferer, yet he did not have 'the patience of an angel' and endurance wore him out:

> What strength do I have that I should still hope? What prospects that I should be patient? Do I have the strength of stone? Is my flesh bronze? Do I have any power to help myself now that success has been driven from me?
> (Job 6:11–13)

There had already been help and advice; after all, Job's friends had come to comfort him in his suffering. At first they were silent with him, contemplating the incomprehensible for seven days and nights. It would remain incomprehensible for Job, but not for his friends. His friends thought he was guilty because such suffering must have its reasons: God is just and does not let anyone be so unhappy without a cause. But Job broke out into a great lament, insisting on his innocence.

Originally, Job had thought as his friends did. He believed that whoever lived a godly life was rewarded for it, and he lived entirely in accordance with this principle of cause and effect. Job was in a pious, transactional relationship with God. The contractual principle – I give to you so that you may give to me – applied completely to Job. Satan had this in mind when he arranged the covert wager with God. He prophesied that Job would renounce God to his face if the contract were no longer honored, if piety were not rewarded. But Job did not renounce God, not even when it was no longer 'only' his possessions and family that were affected. Nor did he when he was sitting in ashes and scraping his wounds during the second attack that Satan delivered with God's consent. His friends did not have such concrete physical experience. They did not know what it meant to suffer so inexplicably in their own bodies. For them, everything remained in the imaginary realm, and only for that general and abstract realm can rules be established. For Job, however, his experience was nothing general but something very specific that affected him personally.

In his physical suffering, Job experienced himself as a unique and irreplaceable individual. No one could take away what happened to him, but it was just in that way that he ultimately found himself. In the encounter with himself, he found an encounter with God that his friends could not imagine. He experienced injustice, indeed a double injustice: on the one hand, his undeserved suffering and, on the other, the unjust accusation of his friends. They believed him guilty and the law to be on their side because they were doing well and Job wasn't.

Just in this experience of injustice, Job gained an astonishing self-assurance. It finally made him call upon God to testify to his innocence against his friends, and Job received that testimony. In the end, God would vent his anger against Job's friends and make them dependent on Job's intercession for them (Job 42:7–9). His friends had not spoken rightly of God, but Job had. That meant –

12. JOB: THE REBELLIOUS SUFFERER

although it went unsaid – that God granted Job's right to complain. But in that complaint, Job had lived out a relationship with God that overcame the transactional nature that had formed the basis of his complaint and his previous relationship with God. In its place, it became a relationship of an emancipated, unconditional faithfulness to God. God was different than expected. God was beyond all human judgment. But Job was also different. He developed something new and unexpected out of everything that was imagined and anticipated. His righteousness in undeserved suffering, which God praised in him before Satan, was transformed into the revelation of a power that only then was actually 'religious'. He did not have to give up God, as his wife suggested, or as other emancipation figures such as Prometheus or Faust had done, to be completely himself and simultaneously in relationship with God. In his new relationship with God, Job went beyond the alternatives of piety or atheism, of believing or not believing. He lived in the tension between rebellion and prayer, which was more honest than the submission demanded by his friends.

The end of the story, however, can strike us as somewhat unsatisfactory. When God responded to Job out of the storm and silenced him by referring to his sublime creative power, the rebellious sufferer gave in, pronounced himself guilty, and repented in dust and ashes (Job 42:5–6), just as his friends had demanded of him. Immediately afterwards, God reversed the situation. He justified Job before his friends and made them dependent on Job's intercession, because, unlike them, Job recognised and knew God. And when Job then interceded for his friends, even though they had hurt him so much before, he got everything back. Indeed, he got back twice as much as he had had before in sheep, camels, cattle, and donkeys. He was given the same number of children as before (although can they really be 'replaced'?), and his daughters were beautiful like no other women in the land. Job lived another 144 years. Then he died 'old and full of life' – a happy ending.

Was everything 'worth it' after all? Was Job yet again rewarded with well-being for his endurance, truthfulness, and recognition of God's incalculable greatness? Was he being rewarded for not holding a grudge against his friends, even though he had just experienced that even the 'righteous' must suffer inexplicably? In the end, would the transactional *quid pro quo* connection be re-established?

That is difficult to say. But in this back and forth between sublimity and transaction, we arrive at an objectivity that goes beyond the alternatives of arbitrariness and law. The transactional connection is a problem: we cannot abandon it, but we must also break through it repeatedly, otherwise there would be nothing sublime in the world.

Transactional tendencies lead just as seductively to an economically self-centered way of thinking as they do in the case of justice. Besides, it is part of the development and individuation of human beings that they do well when they live in a balance of work and wage, investment and return. But this reward does not appear when one is aiming for it or wants to 'pocket' it.

Ultimately, the greatest rewards a person can receive on Earth reside in the deeds themselves, this is what constitutes deeds of love. One gets nothing from them, yet they are themselves a gift. In such deeds, if one may speak so economically here, the effort is already the compensation. The Book of Job does not speak of this. Instead, it questions the transactional context so that its disruption becomes a threshold experience. Job experienced God because he had fallen into misfortune; the 'business model' that had been his guide before no longer worked.

12. JOB: THE REBELLIOUS SUFFERER

It was the experiment that God and Satan arranged with each other that transformed Job. That experiment, which was supposed to demonstrate Job's faithfulness or unfaithfulness, was different from other experiments because what was being examined – the transactional nature of Job's piety – no longer existed in the end. Although in the beginning, Job had basically thought the same way as Satan, by the end, he had freed himself from the captivity of works-righteousness. For this, it was necessary to see into the abyss of God's inscrutability.

Of course, one can argue that the real abyss of the story was the fact that God entered into such an experimental wager with Satan to begin with. If Job had known about it, he would indeed have denied God to his face. Thus, philosopher Christoph Türcke sees as key to the Book of Job that behind the text was an editorial team that deleted the most sensitive part of the story in the interest of the Jewish religion and the canonisation of the Book of Job.[1] As in other ancient oriental fairy tales, Job should have faced a third test, which he would hardly have passed. For Türcke, this is so obvious that it is conspicuous by its absence. Satan must have had a third contact with God, who asked him again, 'Where do you come from?' And Satan would have answered him as before, 'From wandering on the Earth and moving about on it.' And thereupon, God might have said to Satan, 'Have you considered my servant Job? There is no one on Earth like him; he is blameless and upright, a man who fears God and shuns evil. Nor does he hold fast to his righteousness. But you have tempted me against him to corrupt him – in vain.' Türcke continues:

> Satan answered Yahweh and said, 'As long as a man
> does not know God, he may well fear God. But stretch
> forth your hand, and touch his eyes, that it may be made

manifest unto him what we have spoken concerning him. Truly he will curse you to your face.' Then the wrath of Yahweh was kindled against Satan, and he cast him out from his presence.[2]

Thus formulated, God's wrath indicates that Satan would probably have been right. For if Job were to learn that he must suffer thus for the sake of a wager in heaven, then one can imagine that he would not go along with it. But Job did not find out, and that had nothing to do with a guilty secrecy about that imposition on him or an editorial deletion of a supposed third test. Someone else finds out, and not just one person, but the whole world. For we, the readers, know about the agreement between God and Satan, and we witness Job under the conditions of a tremendous test. In its course, he gains self-awareness and independence, which bring him into a relationship with God that is no longer determined by the righteousness of good works.

Nor would he be able to count his suffering as capital that brings him a future bonus. Rather, his suffering is about the great, sublime 'for nothing' – the free relationship, as it prevails both in misfortune and happiness. Against the background of the principle of economy, this extraordinary relationship becomes clear. We see it in Job's behaviour because he learns nothing of the heavenly conditions of his misfortune. If he had known, he would not have been able to develop the freedom in his relationship with God that we witness in him.

13. Judith: Pious Liberator or Temptress?

Martin Luther translated the Book of Judith but he did not include it in the canon of 'his' Holy Scripture. Instead, he included it as an 'apocryphal' text. That probably had to do with the fact that this book involves all too much 'fiction'. Readers encounter all sorts of non-factual things. For example, Nebuchadnezzar was presented as king of Assyria when, in fact, he was king of Babylon. His general Holofernes was most likely not a historical figure, and the fortress of Bethulia was a fictitious place in Israel. The threat to Israel, fictionally summarised here in a single narrative, had spanned over four hundred years.[1]

But this book, with its main character, the beautiful young widow Judith, and her murder of the Assyrian conqueror Holofernes, contains so much tension that it has always moved the emotions, especially of artists. With her great themes of purity and eroticism, autonomy and fear of God, courage and murder, Judith is present in all genres of art as hardly any other Old Testament figure. She appears above all in paintings (Botticelli, Donatello, Cranach, Tintoretto, Klimt, von Stuck, and others) but also in poetry (Hebbel, Nestroy) and music (Scarlatti, Vivaldi).

The story is this. King Nebuchadnezzar had conquered one nation after another, demanding that all those he dominated worshipped him and only him as the true God. The people of Israel had put up unexpected resistance and were reported to have been saved from various dangers and hardships by their faithfulness to God. They, too, were supposed to bow to that demand. However, Holofernes wanted to show that the Israelite God in no way protected them and that there was no God but Nebuchadnezzar.

Therefore, he besieged the city of Bethulia in the Judean mountains with a large number of troops. In so doing, he discovered that he could starve the inhabitants and let them die of thirst without any risk on his side. He could seal off the city from the outside world and destroy the water pipes leading into Bethulia from a spring outside. Then all he had to do was wait.

After almost forty days without water, the inhabitants had reached their limits and were ready to surrender. The council of elders asked for a short period to hold out, in which perhaps God's mercy toward his people would be shown after all. If they were not helped within five days, then they would surrender. The young widow Judith, beautiful, rich, and God-fearing, learned of this. Judith was of good reputation and had lived a very secluded life since her husband's death three and a half years before. She sent a message to the elders, and they came to her.

It is amazing with what self-assurance Judith addressed the elders:

> What you have said to the people today is not right; you have even sworn and pronounced this oath between God and you, promising to surrender the city to our enemies unless the Lord turns and helps us within so many days. Who are you, that have put God to the test this day, and are setting yourselves up in the place of God among the sons of men? (Judith 8:11–12, RSV)

13. JUDITH: PIOUS LIBERATOR OR TEMPTRESS?

Judith demonstrated a very modern, New Testament attitude – that one cannot put conditions on God. There can be no ultimatum that insists God provides his help, and that if he does not, then one is entitled to turn away from him. Judith reminded the old men to be faithful to God, referring to those strong male ancestors, Abraham, Isaac, Jacob and Moses, who remained faithful to God despite great tribulation (Judith 8:19, RSV). One was not to become impatient in suffering but recognise in it a means of God's chastening for one's own betterment. Judith had Job's faithfulness to God, but unlike Job, she saw the city's suffering as God's just punishment. The elders admitted everything to her and even called her a 'devout woman' (Judith 8:31, RSV).

This devout woman then planned a murder to save her people. The contrasts in this story are stark. Judith told no one of her plans and asked the elders to give her a free hand and not inquire into what she was planning. Then she went into her chamber, put on a robe of repentance and prayed. The help for which she asks God is said to be like the help he once granted Moses and the Israelites fleeing Egypt when he drowned their pursuers in the Red Sea.

But this would happen differently than when God himself intervened. Judith then asked God to act *through* her. She lent him her hand and claimed to be the hand of God:

> Give to me, a widow, the strong hand to do what I plan. By the deceit of my lips, strike down the slave with the prince and the prince with his servant; crush their arrogance by the hand of a woman. For your strength does not depend on numbers, nor your might on the powerful. But you are the God of the lowly, helper of the oppressed, upholder of the weak, protector of the forsaken, savior of those without hope. (Judith 9:9–11, RSV)

Judith prayed all this. Whereas a moment before, she had accused the elders of wanting to determine when God should help, she now put forward a plan for God to provide salvation through her by means that are only available to a beautiful woman. Holofernes was to be taken captive by his desire just as the Israelites had been by him in Bethulia, and he was to perish. God would not need the power of an army for this, the erotic power of a woman would be sufficient. Judith had it and offered it to God in loyalty to him.

Was that the prayer of a humble person?

This is what makes the book of Judith so peculiar. We, the readers, are with her in her chamber in her most intimate conversation with God. We cannot be sure – was she the 'devout woman' who did not want to let go of God, even if she had to suffer? Or did she self-importantly declare herself an instrument of God and, in doing so, ultimately arrogate to herself a power with which she placed herself above God? Whose power was it with which she literally rendered Holofernes headless? Was it the power that God had given her in his care for Israel? Did the erotic power of seduction belong to God's saving action?

Such questions probably weigh against Judith on the scales of judgment. On the other hand, what would have happened if Judith had not saved her people from whom Jesus would later be born? This ambiguity is why the Book of Judith is included in the Apocrypha in the 'Book of Books'. Indeed, it is a work of art about which many authors have written, even though Judith remains an anonymous person who can never be traced.

Judith put on make-up and perfume and went to Holofernes' camp in her most beautiful clothes. Impressed by her cleverness and beauty, the Assyrian general was eager to get close to her. He prepared a feast but got so drunk that no sooner was he alone with Judith than he fell asleep. Judith then killed him with his

13. JUDITH: PIOUS LIBERATOR OR TEMPTRESS?

own sword. She left the tent unseen, handed his severed head to her servant, who put it in a linen bag, and returned to Bethulia. The head of Holofernes was presented at the city wall where it was clearly visible.

The leaderless Assyrians then took flight after a harmless but noisy outburst from the Bethulians. Judith was hailed as the 'crown of Jerusalem', the 'delight of Israel', and the 'glory' of the people. 'You have done all this singlehanded,' said the high priest. 'You have done great good to Israel, and God is well pleased with it' (Judith 15:10, RSV). Who was it who acted here?

In a final, prayerful song, Judith thanked God for saving her. Her gratitude oscillated between sovereignty and her submission to divine guidance:

> But the Lord Almighty has foiled him by the hand of a woman. For their mighty one did not fall by the hands of the young men, nor did the sons of the Titans smite him, nor did tall giants set upon him; but Judith, the daughter of Merar'i, undid him with the beauty of her countenance.
> (Judith 16:6–7, RSV)

Her oscillation between humility and self-confident autonomy makes the figure of Judith dazzling. Was she subject to divine guidance, or did she act on her own authority and allow her actions to be justified by the divine's pleasure in them? It could have gone wrong – with her tempting offer, Holofernes could have humiliated her. In any case, she succeeded in her treacherous undertaking, and to that extent she could claim God's approval.

Is there such a thing as pious eroticism? Was the destruction of the enemy with the 'weapons of woman' a thing of God? Was Judith a pious liberator of God's people? Or was she a femme fatale who turned a strong man into a defenceless victim? Questions like these have led to Judith being the subject of extremely contradictory artistic representations.

Roughly speaking, interpretative paths of Judith as a symbol of virtue have led to those of a woman who enjoys her power over a man. In Botticelli and Donatello, she was a political allegory for bravery and the republican will for freedom. In the work of Lucas Cranach the Elder, however, she was given a different note because the painter shows Judith with the head of Holofernes in just the same way as Salome (the embodiment of eroticism) with the head of John the Baptist. However, Cranach shows both women well dressed and adorned more in courtly elegance than radiating eroticism. Only the sword as Judith's attribute distinguishes the two women.

In the twentieth century, Gustav Klimt and Franz von Stuck created paintings that emphasised eroticism. Along the way, the viewer encounters a depiction of Holofernes that asks for our pity, for Judith turned him into a defenceless victim. This is an astonishing mutation. The perpetrator has become the suffering victim, as in Tintoretto and Cristofano Allori.[2]

Yes, there is a pious eroticism, for Judith remained chaste in all her advances towards Holofernes. Yet she was under divine protection:

> As the Lord lives, who has protected me in the way I went,
> it was my face that tricked him to his destruction, and yet he committed no act of sin with me, to defile and shame me.
> (Judith 13:16, RSV)

Judith used seduction without falling into it.

She can, in fact, be the heroine, despite the Renaissance reversals

13. JUDITH: PIOUS LIBERATOR OR TEMPTRESS?

of Holofernes as a victim and the femme fatale interpretations of the twentieth century. Judith can indeed be the woman of a Job-like faithfulness to God, the only one who did not turn away from God in adversity and who would become the model for the Bethulians who wanted to give themselves away in their thirst.

That she acted out of her own strength also gave her something similar to Job. Job's sovereignty lay in the fact that he left behind a transactional relationship and remained faithful to God, even though God withdrew his protective hand from him. Judith held on to the 'suffering-equals-punishment' context, but only to completely dissolve that punishment in active faithfulness. She made faithfulness to God her maxim for action; at the same time, she proved herself completely independent.

Without her independence, the victory over Holofernes would have been worth nothing. God could destroy the Egyptians as the enemies of Israel with his own hand. But he could not have brought Judith and her beauty on her own against Holofernes without abusing her.

Judith was free and pious. That she acted with cunning wraps her in a shimmering veil. That she was also seen as a temptress and self-indulgent about her effect on Holofernes – as in the famous painting by Gustav Klimt – is an interpretation in which the offensive becomes, in turn, a means of lust. Admiration, resistance and fascination are reactions that such a figure deserves, as only a brilliant artistic creation can produce.

14. Jonah the Initiate: Three Days in the Fish

Initiation represents a profound and shattering event in the life of a person. As a result, they are born anew. Paul's Damascus experience was an initiation like no other event reported in the Bible. Such a revolution in the ego manifested as Paul's complete transformation.[1] He went from persecuting the first Christians to becoming their apostle. Other initiatory experiences are less dramatic, and the change accompanying them is less obvious. Peter, for example, was transformed by his repeated failures and experience of guilt after his denial of Christ became fully apparent to him.

Unlike Paul, however, Peter was on the side of Christ from the beginning. The result of his initiation into life was faithfulness to his own Self. It did not mean turning his being upside down, but finding firm inner ground. He needed the experience of his moral downfall to later proclaim the Gospel fearlessly in public against all opposition and before the High Council.

Neither was it the same with Lazarus as with Paul. Lazarus was an intimate friend of Christ. Indeed, he was even especially distinguished since he was the only one of whom it was said that Christ 'loved him'. Was there still a need for transformation there? It seems to be about something else. Lazarus became sick and died, but on the fourth day Christ raised him to new life. Rudolf Steiner

14. JONAH THE INITIATE: THREE DAYS IN THE FISH

has repeatedly described this as an act of initiation which, as was customary in the pre-Christian mysteries, led through a three-and-a-half-day sleep of death. Christ himself carried out that initiation and, at the same time, made an ancient secret public. For Rudolf Steiner, this 'betrayal of the mysteries' was the reason why Christ was then persecuted and executed.[2]

As for Lazarus, he was prepared for his death experience as in the ancient mysteries. In his case, however, that preparation went beyond the usual. There was no longer any need for 'artificial' means, hypnotic or chemical influence, to bring him into that other state, for he had gained insight into the fact that the Logos, the living Word, had become human in Christ. In his death, he experienced the most profound communion with Christ. Brought back to life, he received a new name: John. Rudolf Steiner recognised in him the same person of whom it was said, as before it had been said of Lazarus, that Christ loved him: John the Evangelist, who wrote his Gospel from the most profound knowledge.

The epitome of initiation was the three and a half days in which the human being lost their connection with their physical body. They were as if dead or even, like Lazarus and then Christ himself, actually dead. Paul was blind for three days and did not eat or drink. All these initiates were under the 'sign of Jonah'. Christ explicitly referred to this sign when quite different signs were demanded of him to prove his divine origin. People wanted him to perform miracles of authentication, as the devil did when he tempted Christ after the baptism in the Jordan. But Christ repelled such 'signs from heaven' with strong words: 'He answered, "A wicked and adulterous generation asks for a sign! But none will be given it except the sign of the prophet Jonah"' (Matt. 12:39, cf. also Mark 8:11–13). What Jonah experienced would also happen to Christ:

'For as Jonah was three days and three nights in the belly of a huge fish, so the Son of Man will be three days and three nights in the heart of the earth' (Matt. 12:40).

Whoever thinks of Jonah thinks of the big fish that swallowed him and spewed him out again. He has become the image of an experience of fear and despair that brings one to the brink of death, but from which one is ultimately saved. It is a prophecy that finds its actual fulfilment in the death and resurrection of Christ.

But how does Jonah get into the fish?

Jonah was a singular and atypical prophet. He teaches us not through his prophetic words but through the story he lived through. And it teaches us something we did not expect.

God had commissioned Jonah to announce God's judgment to the people in the city of Nineveh, which had been the epitome of wickedness and a threat to Israel. But Jonah refused the commission and wanted to flee to the other end of the world, to Tarshish (Tartessos) on the southern coast of Spain – out of God's sight, so to speak. The ship he boarded, however, soon found itself in distress due to storms. The ship's crew feared for their lives while Jonah slept in the ship's hold. They first had to waken him to do his duty and pray to his God for salvation. But the crew also suspected that someone had brought these storms upon them through some guilt they had incurred, which was why they were all now in danger. They cast lots to find the culprit, and Jonah was the one. He admitted that he was fleeing from God, which was probably why the storm struck the ship. Resigned, he told the ship's men to throw him into the sea so the storm would subside. The men tried to row ashore at first, but when that failed they threw Jonah into the sea.

Then the Lord sent a large fish, in whose belly Jonah spent three days and three nights. From within the fish, Jonah sang a song of thanksgiving before finally being spat out onto dry land. Jonah had

14. JONAH THE INITIATE: THREE DAYS IN THE FISH

experienced help in the greatest need, recognised God's action, and thanked him for it. So the fish was not the distress, but the rescue from it; not the prison in which he suffered, but the place where he was safe from all danger. In this respect, one can think of the fish as a heralding symbol of Christ. In this image, the fish was not death but life.

Christ himself referred to the fish differently, namely as the grave in which he would lie for three days until his resurrection (Matt. 12:40). Only in this sense of an experience of death could the experience be an initiation. For Jonah, however, it first meant preservation from certain death in the sea.

However – and here two images are interwoven, which makes interpretation difficult – Jonah could not remain in the fish but was spat out again after his song of thanksgiving. This already bore the signature of a new birth. The decisive question about this is: had something changed in Jonah after the three days in the fish so that we can speak of a change of life that allowed him to be born anew? The answer is astonishing but clear: no.

After Jonah's prayer of thanksgiving, God ordered the fish to spit the prophet ashore. He again gave Jonah the order he had previously tried to evade by fleeing. This time Jonah obeyed. He set off for Nineveh, and when he arrived, he said, 'Forty more days and Nineveh will be overthrown' (Jonah 3:4).

That's it. That was all he said. He did not name any grievances and did not call for repentance. He could not have fulfilled his mission more succinctly. Then, as we learn later, he left the city, built a hut outside it, sat down in front of it, and waited to see what would happen to the city (Jonah 4:4–5).

In the city of Nineveh, an amazing thing happened. The stronghold of godlessness paused and came to its senses. Forty days remained – perhaps the disaster could yet be averted. Fasting began, and everyone, young and old, put on penitential garments. The king of Nineveh also took off his purple robes, put on his sackcloth, and lay down in the ashes. They hoped that the God of Israel could still be changed, that he was no longer angry with those who did not want to believe in him. What the people in Jerusalem never did, the Assyrians now did. They repented and turned back, hoping they would be spared but without being quite sure. When God saw that the people of Nineveh 'turned from their wicked ways,' he relented and did not bring on them the destruction he had threatened' (Jonah 3:10). And that was just what Jonah did not like.

In my opinion, the following sentences in the Book of Jonah speak against the widespread view that Jonah's experience with the sea and the fish initiated him. What God did 'seemed very wrong' to Jonah, and he became angry:

> He prayed to the Lord, 'Isn't this what I said, Lord, when I was still at home? That is what I tried to forestall by fleeing to Tarshish. I knew that you are a gracious and compassionate God, slow to anger and abounding in love, a God who relents from sending calamity. Now, Lord, take away my life, for it is better for me to die than to live.'
> (Jonah 4:2–3)

Only here do we learn the real reason why Jonah fled to the other side of the world from the Lord's commission. It was not, as Emil Bock thinks, fear of that great Assyrian city, the 'abode of the monster itself' and of provoking the 'giant's wrath'.[3] Rather, it was his religious worldview that Jonah saw endangered. For him, the enemies of Israel deserve ruin, and he could not understand why they should be pardoned. That is the strange thing: Jonah did not really want the good that he calls the grace, mercy, long-suffering and great goodness of God. At least he did not want it for the Gentiles. He may have been a prophet, but he clung to the old ways. What he encountered was too new, too strange.

But God did not let go. He let a shrub grow over Jonah's hut. 'Then the Lord God provided a leafy plant and made it grow up over Jonah to give shade for his head to ease his discomfort' (Jonah 4:6). But the very next morning, the shrub that Jonah had just enjoyed withered again. The hot wind and sun stung him so severely that he became utterly enervated and would rather have been dead than go on living like that.

Jonah had rejoiced in his own comfort but not in the salvation of the many people in Nineveh. It was that for which God reproached him. God had taken pity on strangers, and he asked Jonah if he thought he was justified in being angry because of a shrub. Jonah was moaning about a plant, and yet God was not supposed to moan about more than 120,000 people and many animals?

Such a question could have become for Jonah a way to self-knowledge that would prepare him for a future initiation. As readers we are put on the track of transformation by this story because we cannot be satisfied with Jonah. In the story, only the people of Nineveh change. They were ahead of Jonah, but just for their being ahead, they needed his prophetic words of impending doom. That is why Christ said to the 'adulterous generation' that demanded a miraculous sign from him:

> The men of Nineveh will stand up at the judgment with this generation and condemn it; for they repented at the preaching of Jonah, and now something greater than Jonah is here. (Matt. 12:41)

15. Tobias: Everything Falls into Place

The Book of Tobit, like the Book of Judith and the story of Susanna and Daniel, is apocryphal. It does not belong to the biblical canon, for it bears many poetic, almost fairy-tale like features. The events it describes 'take place' around 750–600 BC, and it was probably written around 200 BC. Its edifying, doctrinal manner exhorted its early, pre-Christian readers to remain faithful to the law and God. Some of its individual cautionary statements are brittle, but the story itself has its own special charm. The individual destinies of its characters combine to form an unexpected overall composition that 'edifies' us differently than do its moral statements.

The elder Tobit was a Jew who had been led away into exile. During that time he continued to piously serve the chosen people in captivity in Nineveh. Even in a foreign land, he kept the commandments of his people. He did not make himself 'unclean' by eating the Gentiles' food as others did, he admonished his people to keep the commandments, and he courageously buried the Israelites killed by foreign violence, even though it endangered his life. He helped where he could and was the epitome of a merciful man.

As he had about Job, God could have said to Satan about Tobit, 'Have you considered my servant Tobit? There is no one

15. TOBIAS: EVERYTHING FALLS INTO PLACE

on Earth like him; he is blameless and upright, a man who fears God and shuns evil.' Like Job, misfortune befell Tobit after he fell asleep in the shadow of a wall, tired from one of his righteous deeds. Fresh sparrows' droppings fell in his eyes, blinding him (Tobit 2:10, RSV). Was that the reward for his works? To compound his misery, his closest relatives and eventually his wife mocked him.

For the reader, however, the improbability of his misfortune – how could a sparrow's droppings fall so unerringly on a man's eyes? – clarifies that it is just the righteous who are to be tested here. But the suffering initially made Tobit so tired of life that he begged God for the mercy of death.

At this low point in the narrative, the scene switches to another person in distress, namely, the reviled Sarah in Ecbatana, over five hundred kilometers away. She, too, wanted to die because there seemed to be a curse on her. Seven men had been married to her and all had died prematurely on their wedding night. An evil spirit called Asmodeus had killed them (Tobit 3:8, RSV). Sarah's maidservant mocked and insulted her as a 'man-killer'. After that, the reviled woman withdrew, she ate and drank nothing. She asked God to deliver her from her disgrace or take her from the Earth.

Despite the distance separating them, the destinies of old Tobit and Sarah would be drawn together to be resolved through each other. The simultaneous prayers of Tobit and Sarah were heard, and God sent his angel Raphael to join them together for the salvation of all. What seemed nonsensical would turn out to be meaningful in the most beautiful way, but always differently than people expected.

Hoping that his prayer had been heard and that he would soon die, Tobit made his will. He wanted his son and wife to be provided for with the money he had once lent to a man called Gabael.

Tobit had shown charity to Gabael many years ago and had given him, in exchange for a promissory note, a large sum of money. Tobit's son, Tobias, was now to retrieve it and thus secure his own and his mother's future.

Before Tobias set out on his journey, he was given extensive moral instruction on all aspects of life (Tobit 4:5–19, RSV). Since he was still very young, he was to look for a reliable companion for the journey. However, he did not have to look for one because one was already at the door, ready to go. It was Raphael who, when asked by the father, identified himself as Azarias (Hebrew for 'the Lord is mighty'). The man seemed reliable, and the father was pleased. Tobias' dog also accompanied them, and so the son moved between the angel and the beast.

Tobias' mother objected when she realised she was going to be deprived of support in her old age, but his father answered with a trusting remark: 'A good angel will go with him; his journey will be successful, and he will come back safe and sound' (Tobit 5:21, RSV). And that is exactly how things would turn out, even though Tobit could not have known it at the time.

On their journey, young Tobias and his companion came to the river Tigris, where Tobias wanted to wash his tired feet. A big fish shot out and tried to swallow him, but the angel knew what to do. The fish was not to eat Tobias, but the other way round. Tobias grasped the fish by the gills and pulled it out. Its heart, liver and gall were removed and stored, and the fish's flesh used as food for the journey. This is a central motif of the story: what threatens to lead to ruin is turned into success. This applied to the sparrow droppings that caused the father's blindness, it applied to the evil spirit Asmodeus who killed all of Sarah's husbands, and it applied to the fish that wanted to eat Tobias.

After the danger from the fish had been overcome, they needed

15. TOBIAS: EVERYTHING FALLS INTO PLACE

accommodation for the night. Raphael knew that a relative from Tobias' tribe lived nearby in Ecbatana. It was Raguel, the father of Sarah. In her distress, Sarah had prayed for death. But young Tobias now came to make her fortune, which could not have happened if the 'evil' spirit Asmodeus had not killed all her bridegrooms beforehand, thus saving her for the right man: Tobias. Nevertheless, danger continued to emanate from that spirit and Tobias first had to render it harmless.

On Raphael's instructions, Tobias placed the heart and liver of the dangerous fish on burning coals in the bridal chamber to drive Asmodeus away with the smoke. Moreover, instructed by the angel, Tobias knew that he must not touch his bride for the first three nights. These are the proverbial 'Tobias nights' that bring good luck to the marriage, which began with an exorcism and, as a result of abstinence, the devil could not harm it. The most important goal was offspring. The love of children took precedence over the satisfaction of drives, to which all Sarah's other husbands (in the sense of the story, they are 'pagans') had apparently previously fallen prey.

Imagining the stench that fills the wedding chamber from the burning of fish innards seems a little humorous. It is also a little comical that Raguel had a grave dug for Tobias (early in the morning, so people wouldn't notice) because he was worried that Tobias wouldn't survive the wedding night either. But he quickly had it filled in again when he learned that his son-in-law was alive.

The original purpose of the journey was not for Tobias to redeem the unlucky Sarah, but to retrieve the money that Tobit had once lent Gabael. Along the way, however, something other than what was intended happened, and it happened for the salvation of all.

Raphael took care of the further trip to Gabael because the young couple was still supposed to stay with the bride's parents.

Raphael brought Gabael and the money he owed Tobit to Tobias and Sarah so that he could celebrate the wedding.

Meanwhile, Tobias' parents were worried because their son had stayed away longer than expected. Finally, however, the young couple set off for Nineveh. Raphael and Tobias hurried ahead the last part of the way, leaving Sarah to follow them with their servants and cattle. Another creature ran ahead of them wagging its tail – the dog they had taken with them. Only mentioned when the parents were saying goodbye, the dog announced their son's return home. In his haste to take his son back into his arms, the father stumbled, making us aware of his blindness again. But the gall of the fish, which at first represented danger, was then used as a healing ointment: 'and the white films scaled off from the corners of his eyes' and the father saw his son again (Tobit 11:13, RSV).

A week later, Sarah also arrived safe and sound with an entire household and a lot of money, including that lent to Gabael. As in a fairy tale, we have a happy ending.

There was still the matter of rewarding Tobias' travelling companion, who had been so faithful. Both Tobit and Tobias agreed that he should get half of everything. The hour of revelation had arrived and Azarias revealed himself to be Raphael, 'one of the seven angels who stand before the Lord.' On the journey, he had needed no money and had only pretended to eat and drink with Tobias. In reality, he had enjoyed invisible food and drink. He revealed to Tobit that his prayer had been heard and that because he was dear to God, he had had to prove himself in temptation (Tobit 12:13, RSV). Thus, the angel explicitly confirmed the meaning of virtue.

But the story as a whole confirms the meaning of destiny. Because Tobit had been blinded by the sparrow droppings and wanted to die, Tobias was sent to retrieve money lent long ago

15. TOBIAS: EVERYTHING FALLS INTO PLACE

to Gabael; the heart and liver from the fish that threatened to eat Tobias lifted the curse from Sarah by the very man destined for her, and the gall of the fish cured Tobit's blindness. All of this adds up to a whole that is not simply made up of parts that can be added together. Instead, they make up the story of a life in which, as Christian Morgenstern says in his poem 'Silent Ripening', everything falls into place:

> Everything falls into place and is fulfilled,
> One must just be able to expect it;
> Grant years and fields
> For your destiny's evolution.

16. Daniel: A Loyalty Beyond the Reach of Power

In the Old Testament Book of Daniel, some basic concepts of Christianity appear for the first time: the kingdom of God, kingdom of heaven, Son of Man and eternal life. Daniel's narratives and visions of world empires coming to an end and his prophecy of the kingdom of God overcoming the increasingly decadent and ultimately 'anti-Christian' world, go beyond the expectation of a political Messiah who was to restore the kingdom of Israel.

In the last chapter of the book, a time of terrible tribulation is announced, during which Michael, Israel's folk spirit, will overcome the angelic leadership of Persia and Greece. With this, the era of nations will come to an end and a permanent state of salvation under God's rule will be established. In it, death will also be overcome, at least for those who have remained faithful to God and who have been his witnesses in their lives:

> Multitudes who sleep in the dust of the earth will awake: some to everlasting life, others to shame and everlasting contempt. Those who are wise will shine like the brightness of the heavens, and those who lead many to righteousness, like the stars for ever and ever.
> (Dan. 12:2–3)

16. DANIEL: A LOYALTY BEYOND THE REACH OF POWER

This is the earliest passage in the Bible to proclaim the hope of a resurrection of the dead at the end of days, and it is the first and only passage in the Old Testament to speak of 'eternal life'.

This apocalyptic revelation was given to the prophet Daniel, and immediately he was commanded to keep these words under lock and key until the end times. They are only for him, who probably belongs to those wise men who will stand shining like the brightness of heaven at the end. On the other hand, John, the writer of the Book of Revelation, was not to seal his book 'for the time is near' (Rev. 22:10). All were to hear the message that was prepared by Christ's coming and which is then once again witnessed in John's Revelation.

At the time of Daniel – that is, at the time of the Babylonian exile in the sixth century BC – all this is still a long way off. And yet Daniel was promised the resurrection in the book's final words:

> Go your way till the end. You will rest, and then at the end of the days you will rise to receive your allotted inheritance. (Dan. 12:13)

With this end-time perspective, the book stands out from all other Old Testament writings and points far ahead into the time of the New Testament.

Who then is the man to whom the end of time is proclaimed, a time beyond all the worldly rulers he had experienced and those yet to follow? Who is he who shall rest at the end of days? He had led a long and turbulent life in a foreign land for the seventy years of the Babylonian exile. Yet there, at the court of a pagan king, he had remained faithful to his God at every moment, and confirmed him in ever new ways through his actions. Daniel was a politician 'in the world', but not 'of the world' (see John 15:19), a man of God as a statesman. His loyalty lies in the spiritual, which reveals itself in the most earthly conditions.

Daniel was part of an initial group of young men from Israel's upper class whom Nebuchadnezzar had brought to Babylon after his conquest of Jerusalem. He brought them to re-educate them in Babylonian customs, which included matters of food and drink. Daniel and his three friends were to enjoy food and wine from the king's table, but without the king knowing they refused. They did not want to make themselves unclean by eating food in which, through sacrificial customs, foreign gods were involved.

Through the food they chose for themselves, the four young men became stronger and more beautiful. In addition, God granted them special insight and wisdom. In Daniel's case, this gift manifested in him as the capacity to interpret dreams, and it was just this ability that led him to the king's court. Like Joseph with Pharaoh, only the man from a foreign land could interpret Nebuchadnezzar's dream. Not only that, but Daniel was able to enter completely into the soul life of Nebuchadnezzar. He could provide not only an interpretation of the dream, he could also describe the dream itself, which the king had hitherto concealed from his wise men and magicians in order to test them. Thus, Daniel could do what no wise man of Babylon could do and what no one could do 'except the gods, and they do not live among humans' (Dan. 2:11).

But the God of Daniel dwelt with him, and Daniel dwelt with God. After nightly prayer, Nebuchadnezzar's dream was revealed as a statue with a head of gold, a silver breast, copper loins, and iron thighs, and with feet of iron and clay. A stone crushed the statue. Daniel told the king that it stood for four world empires, which would become worse and worse, but that the eternal kingdom of God would come after their destruction. Nebuchadnezzar was

16. DANIEL: A LOYALTY BEYOND THE REACH OF POWER

deeply impressed by the stranger who could tell him both *what* he had dreamed and the meaning of it. In the exuberant gesture of an unpredictable ruler of power, Nebuchadnezzar prostrated himself before Daniel and proclaimed:

> Surely your God is the God of gods and the Lord of
> kings and a revealer of mysteries, for you were able to
> reveal this mystery. (Dan. 2:47)

But then, as if all that had not happened, Nebuchadnezzar had a golden image erected and commanded the people of all nations to fall down and worship it. In the interweaving of religion and politics in Babylonian culture, the worship of the deity was at the same time directed at its representative, the king, presented in that image of gold.

But Daniel's three friends refused to pay homage, even under threat of the most severe punishment – the fiery furnace:

> But if you do not worship it, you will be thrown
> immediately into a blazing furnace. Then what god will be
> able to rescue you from my hand? (Dan. 3:15)

What Nebuchadnezzar had proclaimed as unquestionable – that there was no God above Daniel's God – he arrogantly called into question again by his actions.

But Daniel's friends, in their calm refusal, put the king in his place, for even if they were not saved, they would never worship that image. Their steadfastness was their salvation, which was confirmed by their walking freely and unharmed in the fiery furnace together with a fourth figure who appeared to Nebuchadnezzar like a 'son of the gods' – an angel or perhaps even Daniel?[1]

As arrogantly as he had ordered the harshest punishment for not worshipping his image, so after the rescue of those men did the king enthusiastically praise their God who had saved them from his hand.

This scene shows us two things: first, God's loyalty to Daniel's friends was their salvation in their time of greatest need, and second, Nebuchadnezzar's fascination with the miraculous spectacle shows that such miracles were quite to his taste. In them lay the power that pleased him.

But that still did not prevent Nebuchadnezzar from falling prey once more to his megalomania. For in the interpretation of his second warning dream of a great tree, Daniel would unsuccessfully exhort him to modesty and humility if he did not want to succumb to madness:

> Therefore, your majesty, be pleased to accept my advice: renounce your sins by doing what is right, and your wickedness by being kind to the oppressed. It may be that then your prosperity will continue. (Dan. 4:27)

But Nebuchadnezzar did nothing of the kind. Rather, he referred to great Babylon, which he built into a royal city 'for the glory of my majesty' (Dan. 4:30). Just as Daniel's friends saved themselves through their faithfulness to God, Nebuchadnezzar created madness for himself in his incorrigible megalomania. He let the grace period for humility pass by unused, and so the threat of judgment took effect without further warning. The king fell into madness and ate grass.

But the tide turned again, namely in the moment when he lifted his eyes to heaven. Recognising what was above him, he regained his sanity. In that way, Daniel's God then revealed himself for the third time in the dreams and deeds of his worldly adversary Nebuchadnezzar. In all his arbitrariness and arrogance, the king created an opportunity for Daniel to proclaim and testify to his God.

In the rich narrative of the first part of the Book of Daniel (chapters 1–6), revelation happens through the actions of people. Daniel reported not the great visions in the second part of the book, in which he himself is the narrator, but the deeds of the Gentiles and Israelites that intertwined to form an indirect but no less telling revelation. It occurred in a foreign land and under threat, just the situation in which loyalty could truly prove itself. That also applied to the last two episodes in the book's first part, which report Daniel's deeds entirely in the third person.

Nebuchadnezzar was followed by the Babylonian king Belshazzar. The text speaks of Nebuchadnezzar's son, but he was probably a grandson. Unlike his ancestor, Belshazzar committed an extremely crude sacrilegious act: during a drinking bout, he mocked the God of Israel by misusing the vessels stolen from the Jerusalem temple for his escapades. That outrage was immediately ended by a hand that wrote a mysterious inscription on the wall. Belshazzar turned pale and his legs trembled. No one could interpret the writing except Daniel, who was by then quite old and had fallen into obscurity; only the queen mother remembered him and his abilities. The king promised him purple, gold and power if he deciphered the writing.

'Keep your gifts,' Daniel told him, first reminding him of the consequences of Nebuchadnezzar's arrogance, then interpreting the writing for him. The inscription read: *Mene mene tekel parsin*. Daniel told Belshazzar that God had numbered the days of his kingship. He had weighed him in the balance and found him wanting, and he had divided his kingdom among the Medes and

Persians (Dan. 5:25–28). It was no longer of any use for the king to reward Daniel, even though he clothed him in purple, placed a gold chain around his neck and made him the third highest ruler in his kingdom. That very night Belshazzar was killed. It was a terse ending that punished a carousing, sacrilegious fool with insignificance. The Babylonian empire, made so powerful under Nebuchadnezzar, had ended. But what remained? What remained is God's trace through all worldly empires.

The last episode, which tells of Daniel in the lions' den, also turns his enemy's actions into a revelation of his relationship with God. The Medean king Darius was friendly to him. Jealous officials discredited Daniel because, against the king's interdict, he continued to pray to his God and not to the king. He was punished with seemingly certain death in the lion's den. But no matter what happened, Daniel maintained his alliance with his God. From that unbreakable spiritual bond, he, like Orpheus, was able to subdue the lions. God, Daniel explained, sent an angel who held the lions' jaws shut so that they could not harm him (Dan. 6:22). Happy with the outcome, Darius then explicitly commanded reverence for Daniel's God.

Even at the end of the exile, Daniel was still in the royal court under Cyrus. He had outlasted all those in power. Daniel did not seek power, but his faithfulness to God proved him stronger than all the rulers he served. Even at the end of days, he will remain and will certainly not be found too light. With their power, the kings sought in vain to escape transience. Daniel, in his faithfulness, countered that with an entirely different spiritual duration. Thus, we should not, like Nebuchadnezzar, admire Daniel as the one who could move his God to amazing expressions of power. Daniel perseveres and, in his loyalty, is beyond the reach of power.

17. Dreams Change When Christ Appears

The dreams seventeen-year-old Joseph told his brothers and his father can only be thought of as wishful vanity dreams – his brothers' sheaves of grain bowed before his, and even the sun, the moon, and eleven stars bowed down before him (Gen. 37:7–9). Although they were dreams that caused Joseph's brothers to resent him, they were nevertheless prophetic. But they were only fulfilled after Joseph had undergone profound humiliations.

What is special about the story is that these humiliations occurred because, in telling his dreams, Joseph had made such enemies of his brothers that they threw him into a dry well and sold him to merchants. These and other humiliations were the prerequisites for him to ascend by his own strength to a then 'deserved' elevation entirely corresponding to his dreams. Along that path of destiny he was helped by his ability to interpret dreams. While his own dreams had been all too self-explanatory, those of the cupbearer and the baker whom Joseph encountered in prison required interpretation. Joseph did not claim that art for himself but ascribed it to God alone (Gen. 40:8; 41:16). Joseph could predict the restoration of the cupbearer to his office, but he had to announce the baker's execution. He interpreted without thinking and with a determination that was supposed to testify to his relationship with God. He also interpreted Pharaoh's dream of the fat and lean cows so plausibly that he was promoted as Egypt's second most powerful man. He was thus on the way to fulfilling his boyhood dreams.

The people of the Old Testament were often connected to the divine world through their dreams. Jacob, for example, dreamt of a ladder that stood on the Earth and whose top touched the sky. Angels ascended and descended that ladder, and God stood at the top before Jacob and confirmed his covenant with him, even though he had just tricked his brother Esau out of his first-born blessing (Gen. 28:12–15).

God appeared to King Solomon in a dream and asked him what he should give him. Solomon humbly asked for a listening, obedient heart that knew how to judge wisely and justly. That pleased God and, in the same dream, Solomon was also promised the classic royal gifts of wealth, honour and long life (1Kings 3:5–12). Everything would turn out just as the dream predicted.

The secret of the dream of the Babylonian king Nebuchadnezzar was revealed to the prophet Daniel during the night. Just like Joseph did with the Egyptian Pharaoh, Daniel was able to interpret the Babylonian's dream, which the Babylonian soothsayers and interpreters had been unable to do. Nebuchadnezzar dreamt of a massive statue of gold, silver, bronze, iron and clay being destroyed by a stone, while the stone that smashed the image became a great mountain filling the whole world. That could only mean that God would establish an eternal heavenly kingdom after the earthly kingdoms were destroyed. Impressed and convinced by that interpretation, Nebuchadnezzar prostrated himself before Daniel, acknowledged the God of Israel as supreme, and exalted the Israelite prophet above all the wise men of Babylon (Dan. 2).

17. DREAMS CHANGE WHEN CHRIST APPEARS

Although there were those who warned against prophets who claimed to convey divine messages through their dreams, but were only spreading their own ideas, in the Old Testament the dream was primarily a means of God's revelation, one that became a supporting element of further history.[1] The dream revelation was most effective in Joseph's case, where it intervened in the story like an independent person and became the trigger for action without the dream giving instructions.

In the New Testament, however, dreams are rare and much more meagre. In none of his letters, for example, does Paul attribute the reception of a revelation to dreams. Luke mentions four nocturnal apparitions in Acts that showed Paul the way and supported him in his mission to spread fledgling Christianity (Acts 16:9; 18:9; 23:11; 27:23). But none of these 'dreams' has the opulence and imagery of their Old Testament predecessors. They are more pragmatic, containing direct instructions for action (go there) or spiritual support (do not be afraid).

This is precisely how dreams are structured in Matthew's Gospel, the only Gospel in which dreams are mentioned at all and where only six are recorded. They do not have the revelatory character of those in the Old Testament, nor do they need to be interpreted, for they are clear announcements with which an angel or God himself tells the dreamer what to do.

Joseph, Mary's husband, has four of the six dreams. They all serve to secure Jesus' entry into the world. In the first dream, the angel of the Lord appeared to Joseph to dissuade him from leaving his pregnant bride. He was to name the child she would bear Jesus (Matt. 1:20–21). In the second dream, the angel of the Lord commanded him to flee from Herod to Egypt with Mary and the child (Matt. 2:13). In the third, he was commanded to return to Israel (Matt. 2:19). Finally, in a fourth dream, Joseph was instructed to settle in Nazareth so that the prophet's word of the Messiah as a 'Nazarene' might be fulfilled (Matt. 2:22–23).

After Joseph's first dream, another 'dream of command' was given to the three Magi. After they had offered their gifts of gold, frankincense and myrrh to the infant Jesus, God commanded them not to return to Herod (Matt 2:12). As a result, Herod did not learn of Jesus' whereabouts. Realising he had been deceived, he ordered the cruel infanticide from which the family fled, Joseph having already received his instruction to flee in another dream.

In the beginning, God often intervened in the story of Jesus through dreams. Later, that no longer happened. One can ask oneself whether revelation in dreams became invalid with the incarnation of Christ. When the Word became flesh, alive and effective, a clarity prevailed for which only the alertness of the spirit is adequate. The revelation of God through the incarnation of Christ goes hand in hand with the end of revelations through dreams.

Nevertheless, there also seems to be something in the Gospels that takes the place of Old Testament dreams. These are the parables that Christ told and which, like the dreams, also need interpretation. One must learn to understand them; that is just what one can do through closeness to Christ. Therefore, the disciples should be able to understand the parables, 'Because the knowledge of the secrets of the kingdom of heaven has been given to you, but not to them,' as Christ said when asked why he speaks to the people in parables (Matt. 13:11).

But there is one last dream at the end, one that had a deep meaning. The last dream reported by Matthew is the one that Pilate's wife, a pagan, had that somehow seemed to be aimed at saving Christ from his execution. When her husband was to judge Christ, she sent to him saying, 'Do not have anything to do

17. DREAMS CHANGE WHEN CHRIST APPEARS

with that innocent man, for I have suffered a great deal today in a dream because of him' (Matt. 27:19). It is the Gentile who was still dreaming, but she dreamt discerningly. She saw that Christ was not a criminal but a righteous man. Pilate did not act according to her dream, but when the mob shouted, 'Let him be crucified,' he too asked what evil Christ had done. Then, after he had washed his hands of the matter and thus probably tried to comply with his wife's urging not to have anything to do with this 'innocent man', he let things take their course. Christ went to his death.

Significantly, interpretations of this passage from Matthew go in two opposite directions. Some assume that Pilate's wife's dream came from God (John Chrysostom, Ambrose of Milan and John Calvin all make this claim), while others say it came from Satan (the Venerable Bede, Anselm of Laon and Martin Luther among them).

Those who believe Satan to be the author of the dream assume that Satan wanted to prevent Christ from being crucified according to the divine plan of salvation, for Satan wanted to make the redemption of humankind impossible. Such interpretations suggest themselves to rational-mechanical thinking. We have here the old problem of using evil as an instrument for the sake of the good: as if the murder of Christ were the justified means to the goal of humanity's salvation.

With the dream of Pilate's wife, the 'success' of Golgotha seems once again at stake, this time in the final moments as it were. There is a temptation in the question, 'What would have happened if Pilate had acquitted Christ after his wife's dream?' This question is satanic in reality because it seeks to undo the course of events after the fact, as if everything was still incipient and had not yet happened. It is as if one could arrive at a completely different result by turning a screw already set.

And yet we also need this questioning to recognise freedom in history and to experience that it lies beyond design and arbitrariness, determinism and nihilism. Freedom lies not least in the discovery of meaning. Thus, it is not simply a matter of acting and deciding, but of creatively joining in with what we experience, a kind of singing or dancing along.

It is the task of our time – the time after that of dreams and parables – to do justice to the tremendous paradox of the Gospel by using all the resilience of the consciousness soul. We can no longer assume either God or the devil to be the authors of our soul life, and we certainly cannot expect any instructions for action from them. Pilate's wife had dreamed her own dream. She was not the mouthpiece of good or evil powers. Rather, her dream was a perception of Christ in the form by which she was best able to apprehend it. In her dream, she suffered for one whom others misjudged. In her, the Christ principle shows itself as the essence of individuality.

18. Mary and Elizabeth

Twice within six months, the angel Gabriel announced the unlikely conception of a child. The first time, he announced to the aging priest Zechariah that his prayers had been answered and his wife Elizabeth, long past childbearing age, was to bear a son. The second time, in the sixth month of Elizabeth's pregnancy, Gabriel was sent to a virgin in Nazareth who was familiar to Joseph, a man of the house of David, to announce to her as well the birth of a son: 'and this virgin's name was Mary' (Luke 1:27).

Zechariah doubted that he would become a father, 'I am an old man, and my wife is well along in years' (Luke 1:18). Of course, he would have known that Abraham and Sarah, as well as Isaac and Rebekah, had still had children when that had long seemed impossible. Because of his doubt, Zechariah was made mute until the naming of his son John – a sign of the seriousness of Gabriel's message. Shortly afterwards, Elizabeth became pregnant.

The second announcement was made not to the man but to the woman. In contrast to the elderly Elizabeth, this woman was still a girl, perhaps thirteen or fourteen years old, and was called a virgin twice in one verse (Luke 1:27). She, too, was greeted with 'Fear not' because, in all the extraordinary things that would happen to her, she had 'found favour with God'. Solemnly, Gabriel announced to her the birth of a son:

> He will be great and called the Son of the Most High. The Lord God will give him the throne of his father David, and he will reign over Jacob's descendants forever; his kingdom will never end. (Luke 1:32–33)

That was an incomprehensible announcement. One could imagine fainting in reaction to it. But Mary asked – in a way that was similar to yet different from Zechariah – how that was supposed to be possible. Unlike Zechariah, she did not ask out of a disbelief that asked for a proving sign. Rather, with her question, she opened up the possibility for the angel to explain the unique fatherhood of Mary's son. 'How will this be,' Mary asked the angel, 'since I am a virgin?' That question and the angel's answer lead us into the old difficulty of the 'virgin birth', on which Luke repeatedly places the accent. It cannot and need not ultimately be decided in the sense of a yes or no, for we are moving in a sphere other than that which separates the miraculous from the realistic, namely into the sphere of the sacred. Gabriel replied to Mary:

> The Holy Spirit will come on you, and the power of the Most High will overshadow you. So the holy one to be born will be called the Son of God. (Luke 1:35)

Of course, it makes little sense to think of the announced Jesus, to whom God will give the throne of 'his father David' and who at the same time will only be 'called' God's Son, as someone fatherless in the concrete physical sense. On the other hand, the sonship of Jesus to God was also more than a mere adoption; it

18. MARY AND ELIZABETH

was not choosing a human son to represent him on Earth. This Jesus was God's Son from the beginning, and that means with his conception.

Zechariah demanded a sign as a guarantee of the angel's announcement, whereas Mary asked for nothing of the kind. Instead, she received a significant hint, namely that despite age and infertility, Elizabeth was also expecting a son and was now six months pregnant. The angel concluded his speech with the brief, 'For no word from God will ever fail' (Luke 1:37).

That the seemingly impossible became a reality put Mary completely in relationship with God. Because of her youth, such a thing was perhaps less difficult than for the worldly wise Zechariah and Elizabeth. Mary could stand more easily in relation to God, not as a priestess, but in the purity of her youth. Completely in harmony with God's world, she answered the angel, 'I am the Lord's servant; may your word to me be fulfilled.' (Luke 1:38). Then the angel departed.

After that life-defining encounter, Mary's next step was not, as we might expect today, a conversation or even a hesitant meeting with Joseph, but a journey to Elizabeth, her relative of whom Gabriel spoke. With astonishing determination, the girl set out to visit her aged relative all by herself:

> At that time, Mary got ready and hurried to a town in the hill country of Judea, where she entered Zechariah's home and greeted Elizabeth. (Luke 1:39)

Mary's greeting must have been something that resembled the angel's greeting – an exciting moment that triggered something in Elizabeth, who had kept herself hidden since the beginning of her pregnancy (Luke 1:24). For then it says, 'When Elizabeth heard

Mary's greeting, the baby leaped in her womb' (Luke 1:41). Not only do the two women meet here, but that moment is also the first encounter between John, the forerunner, and the Jesus of the Nathan line of the House of David. In his mother's womb, John is awakened by the encounter.

The onset of the effectiveness of the ego usually happens in the last months before birth as a moment that awakens the whole organism. Here it is not triggered from within John but through contact with another embryonic human being. And that very being, Mary's child, is closer to John than any other. Not only are Mary and Elizabeth related to each other, but also John and Jesus.

Rudolf Steiner speaks of this kinship in his fifth lecture on the Gospel of Luke, where he also reveals the astonishing common origin of the two boys:

> The John ego descended from the same holy region as that from which the soul-being of the Jesus child of the Gospel of Luke descended, save that upon Jesus there were chiefly bestowed qualities not yet permeated by an ego in which egoistic traits had developed: that is to say, a young soul was guided to the place where the reborn Adam was to incarnate.[1]

The 'young soul' means the being of the Nathan Jesus in Luke, and here John is addressed as the reborn Adam.

Also, at the end of the preceding lecture, Steiner speaks for the first time of the two Jesus boys: the royal child of the Solomon line in Matthew and the priestly child of the Nathan line in Luke. He identifies the Nathan Jesus as the re-embodiment of Adam:

18. MARY AND ELIZABETH

Thus the two individualities live side by side: the young Adam-individuality in the child of the priestly line of the house of David, and the Zarathustra-individuality in the child of the kingly line.[2]

So, does the Nathan Jesus contain the Adam soul, or does John? Is the Adam soul in the womb of the pregnant Mary or Elizabeth? He is in *both*, for the two now separated souls of their children were originally one. The encounter of the pregnant women is, at the same time, a re-encounter of the souls of their children in a broader dimension of human history.[3]

The separation of the original Adam soul into two Adam beings, into two sister souls, stands at the very beginning of the development of humanity. It stands at the point where it emerged from mere potential into reality with the actualisation of the ego. The self-centred and egoistic self came into being at the same time. The Luciferic influence turned the virginal 'I' of Adam into a historical 'I' in the sense of an individuality or personality that can develop itself between good and evil. This latter individuality is what incarnated in the pregnant Elizabeth as John. It is the Adam soul *after* the Fall. The Nathan Jesus, however, did not have an ego as John did, one so rich and old in earthly experience. In his lecture series *From Jesus to Christ*, which Steiner gave in Karlsruhe two years after his lectures on the Gospel of Luke, he describes the Nathan Jesus in the following way:

> It was therefore untouched by all Luciferic and Ahrimanic influences; it was indeed something we can think of, in contrast to other human egos, as an empty sphere, still completely virginal with regard to all Earth experience.[4]

At the Fall, this virginal entity, this 'empty sphere', seems to have been separated from the 'I' that entered the world and its history through just that Fall. If Adam also incarnated in the Nathan Jesus, it did so in a resumption of that prelapsarian purity, but it was also in a certain sense deficient. It was not a 'developed ego' according to Steiner:

> But the same ego that was withheld from the Jesus of the Gospel of St Luke was bestowed upon the body of John the Baptist; thus the soul-being in Jesus of the Gospel of St Luke and the ego-being in John the Baptist were inwardly related from the beginning.[5]

In John the Baptist and the Nathan Jesus, the luciferically impregnated but highly developed Adam and the pure original Adam met, as did the two mothers, the elderly Elizabeth with all her life experience, and the innocent young handmaid of the Lord. In Mary's virginity there was, as it were, a state of being parallel to the virginity of the Adam soul, which would now incarnate for the first time. The parallel also existed on the side of Elizabeth and John, for just as John would later recognise Jesus as the Christ-bearer, so his mother already recognised in Mary, her relative, the mother of her Lord. For when the child leapt in her womb, the Holy Spirit also came over her, and she grasped the special pregnancy of Mary:

> Blessed are you among women, and blessed is the child you will bear! But why am I so favored, that the mother of my Lord should come to me? (Luke 1:42–43)

18. MARY AND ELIZABETH

Already in that intimate encounter, the old Adam met the condition for the growth of the new Adam, and that new Adam had his ancestor in the Adam before the Fall. He who had not passed through any incarnations is the reference point of every human being who, through their connection with Christ, is not simply the son or daughter of bodily parents but is, as it were, of 'virgin birth'. This relationship to Christ does not connect them with their parents' germ but with the kingdom of the divine. In this sense, Mary was the first mother to give birth virginally.[6]

19. The Birth of Jesus: Uniquely Atypical

Who was present when the world was created? No one upon whose memory of the event a tradition could be built. There are numerous stories and theories that want to show how it could have been; the myths of different peoples and cultures compete with each other. The creation narrative of the Bible lost its primacy in the nineteenth century and was later replaced by the theory of the Big Bang, although for some the Big Bang theory is also one of these myths.

Creation myths are not based on 'memory'. The creation or emergence of the world did not take place in human history, which is why there are no creation festivals. By contrast, we celebrate the birth of Jesus because we are a part of the human history in which it occurred.

The Christmas story, however, does not remind us solely of the birth of Jesus over two thousand years ago. The Christmas story also includes a wealth of individual incidents, which in turn are full of memories of an even earlier past narrated by the Gospels. At the same time, Jesus' birth is something completely unique and unrepeatable. For many Christmas sermons, this is a difficult hurdle. After all, this 'newness' is now two millennia old. It is therefore often said that Christmas happens again and again, that it

19. THE BIRTH OF JESUS: UNIQUELY ATYPICAL

is a timeless truth. But that only applies to the festival celebration. That which is celebrated – the birth of Jesus – is as unique and unrepeatable as the creation of the world.

Some astronomers suspect that the star of Bethlehem was not unique at all. They claim that it was the so-called Great Conjunction of Jupiter and Saturn, which is repeated at infrequent intervals. The last time these two planets came into complete alignment was December 21, 2020, the next time will be November 4, 2040. Similarly, the story of Jesus' birth is now considered by many interpreters to be a repetition of a particular type of birth – after all, doesn't every semi-divine hero have a 'special' birth?

The circumstances of the birth of a religious founder or semi-divine mythical hero were always accompanied by miraculous signs indicating the beginning of a life that later generations recounted. That was the case, whether it was a dragon slayer like Siegfried or a religious founder like Buddha, Zarathustra or Krishna. Of course, with that observation, the specialness of the birth is suddenly reversed. Despite all the differences in the births of heroes, those special circumstances are so common among them that we are ultimately confronted with something typical – a pattern.

Scholars of comparative religion tend to regard all these birth stories, including the Christmas story, as myths. Myths have no specific place in time: they cannot be dated and they repeat themselves. They are renewed expressions of basic narrative types. They are timeless archetypes.

But the story of Jesus' birth is not a myth. Why? Because it is historical? Did it really happen as we are told?

Let us not make this too easy for ourselves. What chronicler would have recorded it at the time? It would be another thirty years before Jesus caused the kind of sensation that justified such a chronicle in the first place. The story of the star and the stable of Bethlehem and the shepherds in the glow of the Christmas light, the story of old Simeon who was overjoyed to see the promised saviour before his own death, and the story of the wise men from the East and Herod's infanticide – what narrator was present? With which witness was the chain of tradition supposed to have begun? Did Jesus' mother tell her experiences to the disciples thirty years later?

For some theologians, these stories likely arose from the need to make the divinity of the one who died and rose from the dead understandable through a matching birth story. The claim that Jesus was conceived by the Holy Spirit plays a special role in this approach. According to the Nicene Creed, 'by the power Holy Spirit, he became incarnate of the Virgin Mary and was made man.' What must be experienced as problematic in the old creed is today transformed in The Christian Community's creed without losing any of its spiritual significance: 'The birth of Jesus on Earth is a working of the Holy Spirit…'

This working of the Holy Spirit, which does not have to be a 'fathering', involved much more than the physical birth. When we think of the effect of the Holy Spirit, we must think of the circumstances and environment of the birth, including the encounter between the pregnant women Elizabeth and Mary, which was at the same time an encounter between two unborn children, John and Jesus. Or we can imagine all the stories of the Old Testament standing vividly behind the names in the list of ancestors in Luke and Matthew. Jesus' birth was prepared and made possible by all these stories. And the shepherds in the field and the angel who appeared to them were also part of what is called in the creed 'the working of the Holy Spirit'. And the wise men from the East,

19. THE BIRTH OF JESUS: UNIQUELY ATYPICAL

and old Simeon who could die peacefully after seeing the promised saviour, and the successful flight into Egypt and the offering in the temple on Candlemas. And, and, and… We recognise in this series of 'ands' the working of the Holy Spirit as it transforms the rhapsody of individual encounters into a coherent story.

~

The truly dramatic point is that the birth story reveals itself to be incapable of being repeated. It breaks away from the pattern of all other stories of miraculous births in one significant difference: namely the division of *one* birth handed down in two different descriptions in the Gospels, into *two* births.[1]

Until now, the only way of dealing with the differences between Matthew's and Luke's stories has been to see them as a symbolic representation of a real event, or else to dismiss them as pious legend altogether. Taken at their word, both stories contradict each other. If the infanticide led to the flight to Egypt, then the ritual offering in the temple, which had to take place forty days after the birth, could not have taken place. However, the encounter took place there with the old Simeon, who, prompted by the Holy Spirit, came to the temple to acknowledge the Messiah in the child (Luke 2:25–32).

It was not out of some abstract demand to resolve these contradictions that Rudolf Steiner gave his bold depiction of two Jesus boys and two holy families. Rather it was the discovery of a larger, overarching story that brought these separate stories together into a higher unity. It is just this unified story that has been missing from our understanding, one that strives to liberate the truth of the divine from the grasp of a single religion, a single culture, and to bring it to bear universally across *all* cultures and religions.

Through the working of the Holy Spirit, this unique birth stands at the centre of an epic narrative of humanity. It reaches from the Adam soul, part of which remained behind in paradise to be born for the first time in the stable at Bethlehem, to Zarathustra, whose birth was attended by the wise men from the East who had been his disciples in ancient times. The Buddha was also present as the angel who announced the birth of Jesus to the shepherds, and in Simeon we find the reborn Asita, the sage who did not live to see Gautama become the Buddha but who now experienced an even greater fulfilment.[2]

In the meeting between the expectant mothers Elizabeth and Mary, the two Adam souls that had been separated at the Fall met: John the Baptist, the old Adam, and the young Luke Jesus. Through the Fall the old Adam had set the Logos, the Son of God, on the path to incarnation at the Jordan. In the Damascus experience, the soul of the young Luke Jesus would be the light by which Paul recognised the Risen One, which would lead to him later referring to Christ as the new Adam.[3]

This great story is not a new myth because it is not a religion-specific variant of the pattern. The origin of the world can be told in such variants, but the event of Jesus' birth cannot. Unlike the creation of the world, it lies in time. Both creation and Jesus' birth have uniqueness in common, but the uniqueness of Jesus' birth goes beyond the legendary into concrete human history.

20. Moses and John: The Tragedy of the Forerunners

The women in Jesus' family tree mentioned by name in Matthew each had their special history in the Old Testament, and that history always had a certain touch of the 'immoral'. They did not fulfil their task according to the usual custom and order of things.

Tamar, Judah's daughter-in-law, prostituted herself to Judah in order to become pregnant by him because she could not have children through his sons.

Rahab was the harlot of Jericho who hid two of Israel's scouts from her people when the people of Israel took the city. She thus saved herself and found entrance into the foreign nation. She became the mother of Boaz.

And it was to that same Boaz that another foreigner would lay herself at his feet, namely the Moabitess Ruth. Ruth's husband had once come from the land of Judah to her land of Moab because of a famine. As a childless widow, she joined her Israelite mother-in-law to go with her to her homeland. There she found Boaz, by whom she had a son who would be David's grandfather. She became, in unconscious single-mindedness, one of the ancestors of Jesus.

And then there was Bathsheba, the wife of Uriah, with whom David unlawfully united. Eventually – after a first child with Bathsheba died – he would father the later King Solomon with her.

Something earthly in the fullest sense, something all-too-human, coloured and permeated Jesus' prehistory, which became a prerequisite for the incarnation of God. Except for David's behaviour, one cannot speak of guilt but of a 'spicy' genealogy. In it, a single-mindedness prevailed, leading to success by sometimes questionable means. At any rate, this was not how the prehistory of Jesus was imagined. Nevertheless, it seems necessary that the bodily conditions of Christ's incarnation were impregnated with what required redemption as a result of the Fall.

It is quite different with the two great and upright forerunners of Israel and Christ, who played a prominent role in the history of their people and in the incarnation of God: Moses and John the Baptist.

Originally, Moses had not been a bearer of the Israelite mission in any way. On the contrary, after revealing himself to Moses in the burning bush, Yahweh still had to overcome Moses' many resistances to ready him for the fulfilment of his great mission. But once prepared, Moses became a most faithful servant. He took on all trials with almost superhuman strength. He overcame a Pharaoh, led his people through a sea into the desert, and sought the way to the promised land with them for forty years. Repeatedly the people revolted against him; they were rebellious and lacked understanding. But Moses remained loyal to them and to his God, only to end up not reaching the land of fulfilment. At the age of a hundred and twenty, Moses died on Mount Nebo in the land of Moab opposite Jericho on the far side of the Jordan. From there, he was shown the destination of his life's journey, but he did not arrive there.

And John, the other desert man, would also not get to the point of 'It is fulfilled.' He entered his mother's womb as a consecrated man, already filled with the Holy Spirit. According to the archangel

20. MOSES AND JOHN: THE TRAGEDY OF THE FORERUNNERS

Gabriel, who announced John's birth to his father-to-be, 'he will bring back many of the people of Israel to the Lord their God. And he will go on before the Lord, in the spirit and power of Elijah' (Luke 1:16-17). John grew up and became strong in spirit. He lived in the desert until the day he was called (Luke 1:80). Unlike Moses, who was reluctant initially to be called, John was immediately ready. In his short life everything happened quickly, whereas with Moses, who was about ninety years older than John, everything took time. John preached and performed the baptism of repentance or transformation for the forgiveness of sins at the Jordan immediately after his calling (Luke 3:3). In doing so, he drew on the prehistory of the prophets, most notably Elijah, whose fiery demeanour and ascetic attitude John already embodied.

Moses had given his people the law from God's hand; John offered baptism. The one gave a principle from without, the other appealed to inner conversion. While Moses retreated to a mountain to commune with God, John stood far below sea level (around 250 metres or 820 feet) at the Jordan River and baptised all who responded to his call: 'Repent, for the kingdom of heaven is near!' And it was at that deep place that the one who was the whole focus and content of John's mission came to him. Significantly, the location of Christ's incarnation was in the depths. John was the one through whose mediation the 'I am' came fully into the world. This differed from Moses' more elementary encounter in fire and cloud with the 'I am who I am' (Exod. 3:14). That encounter had more of the character of ancient clairvoyance. It objectively corresponded to the kind of revelation of God that in Moses' time did not yet take place entirely on Earth and certainly not in a human body.

The above-mentioned women built upon that body with their unconscious but unerring instinct for the future. With them, the path descended from above, as it were, and fulfilled itself in a way that was as idiosyncratic as it was dazzling. Compared to the women, the two great men were far less successful in their biographies. Their signature was rather that of being left behind. Both were prophets. Moses[1] was the first, John was the last. But just as the one did not cross the Jordan the other did not stand under the cross. Why?

That is difficult to say. John's 'He must become greater; I must become less' (John 3:30), expresses the tragedy of being a herald of something new: to be in the service of what is coming and yet to be so conditioned by the old that you cannot go forward with it. Perhaps with all their prophecy, both Moses and John the Baptist lacked the final insight that lies beyond all laws. The women did not act on the level of the law; instead, they broke through it.

The right relationship to the law is most difficult to find. The law is necessary to regulate our coexistence, and the commandments that Moses received from God to give to the people are still part of the 'ethical minimum' of social life today. They were certainly also related to John, the strict ascetic. He called out to the people 'Metanoeite!' – 'Think differently!' – because it would soon be too late to make up for breaking the law, 'for the kingdom of heaven has come near' (Matt. 3:2). He who would come after him would no longer baptise with water but with the Holy Spirit and with fire. He would 'clear his threshing floor, gathering his wheat into the barn and burning up the chaff with unquenchable fire' (Matt. 3:12). This fire belonged to a vision of the Last Judgment.

What finally doomed John was the only action he performed apart from his baptismal activity. His public accusation of King Herod came from his strict morality. Herod had unlawfully entered into a union with his sister-in-law, Herodias, and for his rebuke Herod had John thrown into prison (Matt. 14:3–4). Not long after that, Herodias' daughter performed a dance for Herod

20. MOSES AND JOHN: THE TRAGEDY OF THE FORERUNNERS

on his birthday. Herod was delighted and swore an oath to give her whatever she wanted. Prompted by her mother, she asked for the head of John the Baptist. Thus, John was beheaded.[2]

Before he died, however, John heard of Christ's work – his healings, his sending of the disciples, and the raising of the dead. John seemed to have expected something else, for doubts came to him and he sent his disciples to Christ to ask him, 'Are you the one who is to come, or should we expect someone else?' (Matt. 11:3). Christ answered:

> The blind receive sight, the lame walk, those who have leprosy are cleansed, the deaf hear, the dead are raised, and the good news is proclaimed to the poor. Blessed is anyone who does not stumble on account of me. (Matt. 11:5–6)

There is no mention of chaff being separated from the wheat and being burned, nor of the axe being laid to the root of trees that do not bear good fruit (Matt. 3:10).

Christ also proclaimed the kingdom of heaven with the same sentence as John did – 'Repent, for the kingdom of heaven is near' (Matt. 4:17) – but it meant something different. It did not simply mean judging the lawbreaker, but the transformation and furtherance of every life. Was that what possibly vexed John? Could he have taken offence at the fact that Christ did not come to punish the unrighteous, that Christ had superseded judgment? One can find this confirmed in the testimony Christ gave of John. In it, he expressed his full respect with one essential qualification. John was more than a prophet. He was the forerunner of the I Am, and among all those born of a woman, none was greater than John the Baptist. But 'whoever is least in the kingdom of heaven is greater than he' (Matt. 11:11).

Moses and John were each the greatest of their time, yet they were not ahead of their time. Instead, they were measured against a future standard for which they were preparing the way but for which they did not, and could not, yet have any understanding. Expectations for them were greater than those of others because they were already on a higher level of development. They then paid tribute to this by remaining behind – outside the promised land, and behind Christ. This is what John meant when he said, 'He must become greater; I must become less' (John 3:30).

21. Appearances of God

The Epiphany traditionally refers to the manifestation of God through Christ to the Magi. But there are other epiphanies recorded in the Bible where God makes his presence known to human beings. God appeared many times to Abraham, for example, and addressed him repeatedly. He asked Abraham to leave his homeland and move to another country. He made a covenant with him, which was marked by changing his name from Abram to Abraham and by establishing the rite of circumcision. God also announced that the ninety-nine-year-old would father a son, Isaac, and that God would keep his covenant with Isaac and his descendants (cf. Gen. 17).

One of God's epiphanies to Abraham could hardly be more concrete:

> The Lord appeared to Abraham near the great trees of Mamre while he was sitting at the entrance to his tent in the heat of the day. Abraham looked up and saw three men standing nearby. When he saw them, he hurried from the entrance of his tent to meet them and bowed low to the ground. He said, 'If I have found favor in your eyes, my lord, do not pass your servant by. Let a little water be

brought, and then you may all wash your feet and rest under this tree. Let me get you something to eat, so you can be refreshed and then go on your way – now that you have come to your servant.' 'Very well,' they answered, 'do as you say.' (Gen 18:1–5)

Even if Abraham did not immediately recognise who was meeting him in the form of the three men, it is clear to the reader that he had God as a visitor, for the narrator begins his story with 'The Lord appeared to Abraham...' It is unclear whether God appeared here with two companions or in the threefold nature of all humans so that, as the Church Fathers later saw it, one could already find the mystery of the Trinity hinted at here. In any case, references to the three fluctuate between the plural and the singular. At one point, *they* say to Abraham, 'Where is Sarah, your wife?' and immediately afterwards it says in the singular, 'I will surely return to you about this time next year, and Sarah your wife will have a son' (Gen 18:9–10).

Sarah, hidden behind the door of the tent, laughed when she heard this. 'After I am worn out, and my lord is old, will I now have this pleasure?' she said to herself. But although what she had said was not meant for the ears of their guests, nevertheless it had been heard by him who hears all:

> Then the Lord said to Abraham, 'Why did Sarah laugh and say, "Will I really have a child, now that I am old?" Is anything too hard for the Lord? I will return to you at the appointed time next year and Sarah will have a son.'
> (Gen 18:13–14)

Nothing is impossible for the Lord.

21. APPEARANCES OF GOD

Later, the archangel Gabriel would say something similar to Mary when he announced that she was to have a son (Luke 1:34–37). Sarah, the eavesdropper behind the tent door, was caught out laughing and only then realised who was standing outside the door. She had an epiphany. But she did not yet understand how to deal with it. In what she did next, she confirmed God's appearance and denied it at the same time: 'Sarah was afraid, so she lied and said, "I did not laugh." But he said, "Yes, you did laugh."' (Genesis 18:15). The proclamation of a son must be correct, for it came from one who could see into a person's secrets. At the same time, however, that very thing was uncanny, and Sarah was afraid of God's presence, just as Adam and Eve were when God appeared to them after the Fall and they hid from him.

~

Another well-known epiphany is found in the story of Jacob's struggle at the Jabbok River (Gen. 32:22–30). Jacob was on his way back to his homeland. He knew he would meet his brother Esau, whom he had cheated out of his birthright. Jacob had prepared well for that difficult meeting. Along with gifts, he had brought his family, workers and flocks. He remained alone at the ford of the Jabbok. During the night, a stranger surprised him. He wrestled with Jacob until the early morning, but neither could defeat the other. Jacob received such a violent blow on the hip that he would limp for the rest of his life, but he did not give up. Instead, he demanded something from his opponent, whom he sensed to be a very special being. He demanded a blessing. 'I will not let you go unless you bless me' (Gen. 32:26). Struggle and blessing were intertwined in that encounter. Both fighters were decisively connected. God and a human being met in them, wrestling for the future of Israel. Certainly, one could also think of an angel of

God fighting with Jacob, but that would be less compatible with the renaming of Jacob as Israel (God fights for us, God fighter). Furthermore, Jacob's epilogue at the end of the scene seems to refer to a dramatic encounter with God, because from then on he called the place of the event Peniel, which means 'face of God' because he saw God face to face 'and yet my life was spared' (Gen. 32:31).

~

Moses had an encounter with God in the burning bush that determined the rest of his life (Exod. 3). While tending his father-in-law's sheep he came to the divine mountain Horeb. There he saw a bush on fire, although the bush itself did not appear to burn. As Moses drew closer to investigate, God spoke out of the fire: 'Do not come any closer. Take off your sandals, for the place where you are standing is holy ground' (Exod. 3:5). Moses' curiosity was aroused by what he at first thought was a natural phenomenon; he did not immediately see in the fire a divine revelation. God revealed himself to Moses as the God of his fathers, at which point Moses covered his face for fear of seeing him. He was then given his lifelong mission to lead Israel out of bondage in Egypt into the land flowing with milk and honey.

At first, Moses hesitated to accept the mission at all. Then he wanted to know the name of God so he could authenticate his mission before the people of Israel, for there were many gods in the world of those times. That name had a special meaning. It is a whole sentence in the centre of which stands the 'I'. 'I will be who I will be' or 'I am who I am' or – as Rudolf Steiner accentuates it, 'I am the I Am.' In his essence, this God is the I-being. With him, the 'I' came into the world. And it is just this revelation of the 'I' in the world that then passed completely into world history in the events of Palestine. According to Steiner:

21. APPEARANCES OF GOD

No godhead other than the Christ is intended to be introduced by the words 'I am the I Am'. The God who later appeared in the human body and who confronted humanity with the Mystery of Golgotha reigns invisibly after he announced himself earlier in the fire element in nature, in the burning bush and in the lightning fire of Sinai.[1]

Against the background of that special appearance of Christ, but also against that of other epiphanies, we can now ask: why do we also call the baptism in the Jordan, in which Christ united with Jesus, an epiphany – an appearance of God?

Originally, in the second century, the Gnostics valued Jesus' baptism in the Jordan in a similar way to its value in anthroposophy today. Thus, as Peter Selg has found out, an Epiphany festival commemorating the baptism was founded even before a Christmas festival celebrating Jesus' birth.[2] Despite this, however, the idea of the incarnation of Christ in Jesus was alien to them. They thought of the connection between Jesus and Christ more as an external and temporary one, which in no way lasted until his death on the cross.[3] For the Gnostics, Christ was a spiritual being who did not suffer. Since they believed that Christ's connection with Jesus was only temporary, and further that his appearance in a physical body was only apparent and not actual, more illusory than anything else, it is understandable that the event the Gnostics chose to mark this is called 'Epiphany': an appearance.

Then there was the historical weakening of that baptism event in the fourth and fifth centuries by fixing Christmas on December 25, commemorating the birth of that special child, Jesus. January 6, the date of Epiphany, came instead to mark the adoration of the three Magi, rather than Jesus' later baptism. When we speak of 'appearance' in this context, that fits well with the light of the star that led the wise men from the East to Bethlehem. After all, they were thought of as 'Gentiles'. Jesus Christ also appeared to them. This formed the core of the feast of the Epiphany.

The mystery of the incarnation of Christ is not an issue here. For that event, the talk of an 'appearance' does not fit. What 'appeared' at the Jordan in connection with the incarnation of Christ was the dove and the voice from heaven: 'You are my beloved Son, today I have begotten you' (Luke 3:22). The dove and voice disappeared again as they did at other epiphanies. They are like a short-lived visitation in various guises. Christ, however, was not visiting but becoming flesh – whether we speak of the Jordan baptism as his birth or as his begetting. His incarnation meant the complete penetration of the body of Jesus down to the bones.

Sometimes names do play a role – as with the name of God, 'I Am'. But perhaps January 6 should be given a more appropriate name, one that we don't just use out of habit. It could be called the Feast of the Incarnation. The incarnation was completed on Golgotha, which is connected with the resurrection. Side by side, these two feasts take precedence over all other Christian festivals.

22. Nicodemus: On the Threshold of a New Birth

The 'cleansing of the temple' caused a stir. Christ drove cattle and sheep out of the temple with a scourge made of cords and overturned the merchants' tables because he did not want the house of God to be turned into a marketplace. The Jews asked where he got the right to do this: 'What sign do you show us that you may do this?' They received an answer that was incomprehensible to their everyday understanding: 'Destroy this temple, and in three days I will raise it up' (John 2:18–19). The temple had taken forty-six years to build; it would be impossible to rebuild it in just three days. Only after the resurrection did it become clear to the disciples what Christ had been meant: it was the temple of his body that was to be rebuilt after three days.

The misunderstanding is significant. In retrospect, one can well say how Christ's words were 'actually' to be understood. At the time, however, the claim that the temple could be rebuilt in three days caused confusion. But the confusion was constructive, it was an opportunity to press for a deeper understanding. Christ could not have meant what he said in the way the Jews understood it. How then *did* he mean it?

This was a question that Nicodemus may also have asked himself. He would seek out Christ soon afterwards. He wanted to know more precisely who the man was who performed signs that no one else could do 'if God were not with him' (John 3:2). Nicodemus was a member of the High Council. He was one of the rulers, a scribe who sensed that there was something extraordinary about this man. Nicodemus was distinguished by the fact that, as an individual, he left the collective of the scribes to learn something new.

That he came to Christ 'in the night' has been given many different interpretations. Some commentators believe that Nicodemus was a sympathiser of Christ, unlike the other elders who opposed him. Nicodemus sought to talk to him in secret, under cover of darkness, because he was afraid of his colleagues and for his position if he were to approach Christ publicly and get involved with him.

Rudolf Steiner dismissed that as the most trivial explanation imaginable. The phrase 'by night' meant rather that Nicodemus came to Christ in a nocturnal clairvoyant state that human beings can achieve only outside their physical and etheric bodies, outside of their daytime consciousness.[1]

That this was an extraordinary situation that did not belong in the materiality of daily business was made clear by the fact that the most crucial question for a person's life hovered in the room without being voiced. Thus, Nicodemus did not explicitly ask, 'What must I do to enter the kingdom of God?' Christ nevertheless answered that 'no one can see the kingdom of God unless they are born again' (John 3:3).

This being 'born again' is the transition from the world of the senses into the world of the spirit. It has the same quality as rebuilding the temple in three days and is equally in danger of being misunderstood. But that danger, of which Nicodemus was presumably aware, is like a signpost that draws all attention to the very otherness of Christ's speech.

22. NICODEMUS: ON THE THRESHOLD OF A NEW BIRTH

This became clear in Nicodemus' supposedly naïve question: "'How can someone be born when they are old?" Nicodemus asked. "Surely they cannot enter a second time into their mother's womb to be born!'" (John 3:4). Of course they could not, and Nicodemus knew that. It was as impossible as rebuilding Solomon's temple in three days. His question related entirely to the physical realm. But it was just through this absurd question that Nicodemus paved the way for the spiritual explanation in Christ's next answer.

Christ distinguished between birth in the flesh and birth through the spirit. He understood that Nicodemus was asking him about the new birth of which he had spoken. Christ explained it with the metaphor of the wind that blows where it wills: the wind can be heard, but one cannot say 'where it comes from or where it is going' (John 3:8). Someone born again is born of 'water and the spirit'. They receive the spirit of God in baptism. They cannot bring that about themselves; it is as inaccessible as the wind, which we cannot powerfully set in motion nor direct ourselves. Yet we can still do something. Like Nicodemus, we can ask.

Christ paid complete attention to him, and only the night provided the right atmosphere for that attention. Just as the study of the Torah at night has a special intensity, so also Nicodemus' nighttime conversation with Christ had a special concentration and intimacy about it. He was a sincere questioner about the threshold to the kingdom of God, the threshold between life in the flesh and life in the spirit.

Nicodemus' misunderstanding served as a spur to a higher comprehension, even though, as a scribe, he might have been expected to already know what Christ meant: "'You are Israel's teacher," said Jesus "and do you not understand these things?"' (John 3:10). Nevertheless, Nicodemus came to understand and experienced the new birth. This was evidenced later by his undisguised advocacy of Christ in the High Council (John 7:50) and later still by his presence in the care of Christ's body. The fact that he honoured the one who had been crucified like a criminal with a royal quantity of anointing oil was his clear acknowledgement of Christ (John 19:39).

Nicodemus had been blown by that wind of which Christ said it 'blows wherever it pleases. You hear its sound, but you cannot tell where it comes from or where it is going'. (John 3:8). Nicodemus had heard it clearly, and therefore much was expected of him. The crucifixion's effect of salvation had already been proclaimed to him in the nighttime conversation: 'Just as Moses lifted up the snake in the wilderness, so the Son of Man must be lifted up, that everyone who believes in him may have eternal life' (John 3:14). It was a cryptic saying that prophetically compared the lifting of the serpent in the desert to the 'lifting' of Christ on the cross, and just as that first event had a healing effect on the Israelites, so would the resurrection that followed Christ being lifted up on the cross have a healing effect for all humanity. Such momentous occurrences could only be understood gradually and at the proper time. Nicodemus' questioning led him into a circle that made him pregnant with his own new birth.

23. Christ and the Samaritan Woman

Young Rebecca, who would become Isaac's wife, had revealed her nature at the well. Abraham's servant, who had been sent out as a marriage broker, had asked her for a drink when she came in the evening with other women to draw water at the well outside the city. 'Drink, my lord!' Rebecca said to him, and when he had drunk she also drew water for his camels (Gen 24:18–20). It all happened quickly, without conversation, just as the situation demanded. Rebecca was beautiful, young and innocent, and she did what was necessary.

One can contrast this meeting with Christ's encounter with the Samaritan woman at Jacob's well in the Gospel of John. 'Will you give me a drink?' Christ said to the woman (John 4:7). He was tired from his journey. It was hot, for it was around noon, and the well was too deep to draw from without a suitable vessel. But instead of giving the thirsty man a drink, the woman pointed out to him:

> 'You are a Jew, and I am a Samaritan woman. How can you ask me for a drink?' (For Jews do not associate with Samaritans.) (John 4:9)

Here, too, the nature of the woman at the well revealed itself, but differently from Rebecca and not at first to her advantage. She came alone at midday, not with the other women who came in the morning or the evening. Presumably, she was not particularly popular. Moreover, she was a Samaritan, a group of people who were descended from the ancient Israelites but who mixed freely with pagans. At the time of Christ, the Samaritans were considered by the Jews to be heretics. The Samaritans only recognised the five books of Moses and not the other canonical scriptures, and they had their own holy temple on Mount Gerizim, which they had built when their offer to assist in the building of the temple in Jerusalem was rejected.

The situation was thus 'unseemly' in many ways. The very fact that a Jewish man – and a rabbi at that – was talking to a woman was inappropriate. The disciples also wondered about it when they came to the well after buying food in the nearby town (John 4:27). Furthermore, we learn that the Samaritan woman had already been married five times and was now in an illegitimate relationship with a sixth man (John 4:18). She could not have been young and innocent like Rebecca; she had life experience.

The Samaritan woman did not give Christ a drink. She left as soon as the disciples appeared, leaving behind her unfilled jar. She went to tell the other Samaritans about her encounter because she had experienced something incredible with the man at the well – quite unexpectedly, she might have met the Messiah. Presumably, she would return. The jar she left behind could be seen as the not-so-unconscious pledge she left with Christ at the well.

The Samaritan woman referred with a certain pride to drinking from Jacob's well (John 4:12), and she was clearly thinking of earthly water when Christ asked her for a drink. When the woman questioned the appropriateness of a Jew asking a Samaritan for

23. CHRIST AND THE SAMARITAN WOMAN

a drink, Christ replied: 'If you knew the gift of God and who it is that asks you for a drink, you would have asked him and he would have given you living water' (John 4:10). But she did not yet recognise him or did not yet *want* to recognise him. Instead, she challenged him to further explanations: 'You have nothing to draw with and the well is deep. Where can you get this living water? Are you greater than our father Jacob?' (John 4:11–12). Indeed, this 'greater' is what the conversation between Christ and the Samaritan woman is about. Neither of them would drink water from Jacob's well, which would only make them thirst again, but the 'living water' that Christ could give the Samaritan woman would do its work. Somehow it seems to flow in this conversation and transform the Samaritan woman.

Some interpreters of this story see a certain spitefulness in the Samaritan woman's behaviour, in the way she withholds water from a thirsty Jew who, she believes, disregards her people and perhaps her in particular.[1]

But the whole aura of the scene seems to suggest otherwise. This Samaritan woman was an experienced woman who knew her way around life and men. She had no inhibitions about opposing them but was at the same time curious. She sensed the specificity of the situation, and was open to a new experience.

A conversation between two strangers can blossom from openness. They say things to each other that are completely focused on the essential. It is anything but small talk. At the same time, there can also be an erotic glow over the scene. Here it did not involve lust but a higher recognition. Christ and the Samaritan woman recognised each other in their deepest being. For this, taboos had to be broken. Neither of them had a problem with this. They were both free of conventions and clichés. Indeed, it was part of the creativity of their lives.

Christ also broke a taboo in another place with a Samaritan, namely in his story of the Good Samaritan. Asked by an expert in the law about the essence of charity and what he must do to attain eternal life, Christ explained that a stranger can also be our neighbour, even the Samaritan despised by the Jews. The neighbour is not a fellow believer who follows the same rules, but a person independent of affiliations. Thus, as is well known, it was the outsider, the Samaritan, who rescued and cared for a stranger who had been attacked by robbers and beaten half to death (Luke 10:25–37). 'Eternal life' is not reserved for the elect. The old differences became meaningless before the greatness of that 'gift of God' that the Samaritan woman at the well was to recognise (John 4:10).

The Samaritan woman did not give Christ a drink, but she met him in another way. With her questions and answers, she revealed Christ's saving nature. Through a potential misunderstanding she sought to clarify the higher meaning of Christ's source of life: 'You have nothing to draw with. Where can you get this living water?' This makes it clear that the 'living water' is about something quite different from what is welling up from the depths of Jacob's well. The Samaritan woman's request for Christ to give her some of this 'magic water' so that she wouldn't have to got to the trouble of drawing water from the well in future, shows that she already had some idea that this man had something quite different to offer. The Samaritan woman did not behave submissively in any way. Was it only because she did not yet know who she had before her? Perhaps, but she was completely sincere with the stranger and beyond posturing humility. That is not to say she was disrespectful. She had the courage the disciples lacked when they did not dare ask Christ why he was talking to a woman in such an improper manner (John 4:27).

23. CHRIST AND THE SAMARITAN WOMAN

Then Christ changed the subject and asked the woman to fetch her husband, but his manner of speaking had something in common with the way the Samaritan woman had spoken – they both knew that there was a hidden meaning in what they said. The women replied that she had no husband and Christ said, 'You have had five husbands, and the man you now have is not your husband' (John 4:18).[2] The Samaritan women felt recognised by this man and, gradually, she began to recognise him.

First, she said to him, 'Sir, I see that you are a prophet' (John 4:19). As a prophet, as one who must know, she asked him who was right: the Samaritans who worshipped God on Mount Gerizim or the Jews who did so in Jerusalem. In the beginning, she had stated that the Jews had no fellowship with the Samaritans, which was an expression of her astonishment at being addressed by a Jew. Now she was prepared to concede to that Jew a decision about the proper place of prayer, but perhaps she suspected that was not the point. Christ did not answer her question directly, instead he spoke of a time that had already come when 'the true worshippers will worship the Father in the spirit and in truth' (John 4:23). That promise applied to all.

However, even though Christ is the 'living water' that has been made available to all, as an incarnated being he still depended on earthly water, the kind that had to be drawn from a stone-lined well. Similarly, although God is spirit and those who worship him must do so in spirit and in truth (John 4:24), Christ's path of incarnation was through God's 'chosen' people: 'for salvation is from the Jews' (John 4:22). That was the road Christ took.

The meeting between Christ and the Samaritan woman was an event for both of them because she also prepared the way for him. When the Samaritan woman said to him, 'I know that Messiah is coming. When he comes, he will explain everything to us,' that was Christ's prompt to make himself known: 'I, the one speaking to you – I am he' (John 4:25–26). He who was to come had arrived. He was standing right in front of her. That was the climax of recognition.

What followed then was the conclusion. The disciples appeared with their food, but they could no longer disturb the intimacy of the revelation. The decisive point had been made. The woman left her water jar, went into the city, and became a fountain of living water: 'Come, see a man who told me everything I ever did. Could this be the Messiah?' And they came and recognised him themselves and asked him to stay.

24. Simon Peter: Courage and Weakness

One can be surprised that Samson, the adventurer with such great physical powers and desires and equally great weaknesses, became one of the twelve judges of Israel. Likewise, one can also be surprised that fickle Simon Peter became one of the twelve disciples and, what is more, the one who is mentioned most often and emphatically as the first one called (Matt. 10:2).

However, Samson and Simon are two ambivalent figures who belong in a particular way to each of those twelve. This distinctive calling of such fallible characters is a signature of the Old Testament, where we also find complex figures among Jacob's twelve sons. Such characters are also found in the New Testament. This gives us confidence that even someone afflicted with a great many weaknesses can still be completely connected with the heavenly. The fact that the keys of heaven are placed in the hands of such a temperamental risk-taker as Simon Peter should not make us fearful. On the contrary, we learn the trust that Simon Peter would have liked to have had, but which he yet lacked, when he attempted to walk on water.

After feeding the five thousand, the disciples sailed together across the lake. Waves rocked their boat. Then they saw a figure coming across the water and were afraid, for they thought it was a ghost. But it was Christ: 'Take courage! It is I. Do not be afraid.'

To know salvation in a fearful situation all at once gives wings to the soul, and Simon Peter, in his enthusiasm, cried out to Christ, 'Lord, if it is you, tell me to come to you on the water.' As one says to a child ready to take their first steps unaided, 'Come here!' so did Christ to Peter. And Peter found that he was able to. But then he felt the wind, and he became aware of the miracle of his walking on the water and that was it. He started to sink and cried out for help. Christ took him by the hand and said, 'You of little faith, why did you doubt?' (Matt. 14:25–31)

With the awareness of the miracle, doubt began, and thus what could have succeeded became something impossible. Peter, who would only later receive that name, was the rock that sank. His strength was also his weakness. His trust and his knowledge of God were greater than those of the others, but so was his doubt when it came upon him. Peter stepped out of the circle of disciples, but he also fully represented their inadequacy. With his eyes fixed on Christ, he dared the impossible, only to completely lose his footing as a result of his all too earthly self-consciousness.

Peter wanted to but could not yet. That was his distinction. Like Samson, he stood out and yet failed. And just as Samson finally betrayed the secret of his strength-giving hair and thus his connection to God, so Peter, for all his faithfulness, would nevertheless deny Christ when the danger became too great and he feared for his life. Samson was a forerunner and Simon Peter a passionate disciple of the Lord, but impulsiveness belonged to them both. They were fiery, and they flamed out. They may have been singularly chosen for that very reason: Samson already from his mother's womb (see Chapter 8), and Simon as the first among the disciples, whose specialness perhaps lay in his exaggeration of what is so typically human.

24. SIMON PETER: COURAGE AND WEAKNESS

Peter was torn between heaven and Earth like no other. He would have been entirely ready for heaven were it not for the mortal danger of having to leave the earthly. Time and again, it was fear that caused the courageous and insightful man to buckle. The scene on the lake typified Peter. He rushed to meet Christ but was muddled by his own courage and its consequences, he became faint hearted.

The central passage in the Gospels – the so-called confession of Peter, which should really be called Peter's recognition of Christ – also bears witness to that basic trait in his nature with his subsequent defence against suffering. When Christ asked the disciples who they thought he was, Simon Peter answered, 'You are the Messiah, the Son of the living God' (Matt. 16:16). In response to that direct and unerring testimony, Christ distinguished him by a personal adulation. He acknowledged Peter's openness to God's revelation: 'This was not revealed to you by flesh and blood, but by my Father in heaven' (Matt. 16:17). Then Peter was given his name combined with a promise of a future beyond his present powers into which he must first grow: 'But I say to you, you are Peter (*petros*) and on this rock (*petra*) I will build my church (*ekklesia*, literally the ones called out), and the gates (*pylai*) of Hades will not overcome it' (Matt. 16:18). The powers of death will not be able to prevail over the people of God (*ekklesia*). But the fact that the powers of death even exist and that they are not first eliminated before they have to be suffered is incomprehensible to Peter.

Human and divine opinions differ on the understanding of death. For Peter, death was the enemy, something to be feared; for Christ, it was a transition to a higher form of existence. These opposing directions collide at the central point of Peter's confession and Christ's following announcement of his Passion. Here is the sudden reversal in the drama.

Everything was going well. Then:

> From that time on, Jesus began to explain to his disciples that he must go to Jerusalem and suffer many things at the hands of the elders, the chief priests, and the teachers of the law, and that he must be killed and on the third day be raised to life. Peter took him aside and began to rebuke him. 'Never, Lord!' he said. 'This shall never happen to you!' Jesus turned and said to Peter, 'Get behind me, Satan! You are a stumbling block to me; you do not have in mind the things of God, but merely human concerns.' (Matt. 16:21–23)

Peter's rejection as Satan followed his recognition of Christ because he did not understand Christ's mission.[1] These are the two aspects to Peter's soul: the highest openness to revelation on the one hand, and the deepest lack of understanding on the other. But can we blame him for that? How can one easily understand the meaning of suffering and death so that one does not object to them? Didn't Peter mean well by Christ when he wanted to save him from the worst? And can we not also understand him when he drew his sword and cut off the high priest's servant's ear to prevent Christ's arrest (John 18:10)?

For Christ, however, it was just in that desire to save that the danger lay, and against which he must defend himself: 'Shall I not drink the cup which my Father has given me?' (John 18:11). Not to drink it would be to fall into Satan's hands. That was the temptation that had existed since his baptism in the Jordan. Not wanting to live through death was the danger that would prevent salvation, something Christ declared immediately after he had rebuked Peter:

24. SIMON PETER: COURAGE AND WEAKNESS

Whoever wants to be my disciple must deny themselves and take up their cross and follow me. For whoever wants to save their life will lose it, but whoever loses their life for me will find it. What good will it be for someone to gain the whole world, yet forfeit their soul? (Matt. 16:24–26)

Did Peter understand that teaching? Perhaps he did. Or perhaps, though no one else was as good willed as he, he had not yet managed it.

When Christ announced at the Last Supper that he would be betrayed by one of the disciples and that all would eventually take offence at him, Peter firmly rejected this: 'But Peter declared, "Even if I have to die with you, I will never disown you."' (Matt. 26:35). But we know that that was just what he would do. In his theoretical readiness to surrender, Peter could not cope with the life-threatening seriousness of the situation. No one else was as shaken by that as he. The crowing cock brought his deed into consciousness, and he wept bitter tears of remorse.

In Peter, we see how difficult it is not only to understand the mystery of death and resurrection, but to make it entirely our own. Peter was caught between his courage and weakness, his knowledge and blindness, his recognition and denial. We see all of that firsthand. In this, he was perhaps much closer to us than his later like-minded contemporary, whose proverbial transformation from Saul to Paul was almost seamless. Peter is quite rightly the first and outstanding disciple because we can experience in him the struggle of becoming a Christian. The other first disciple, Christ's beloved disciple, had gone through his special initiation earlier, while Peter came to his only through a life-initiation. Lazarus-John had gone through a transforming death, while Peter long shunned his. In the beloved disciple, everything that was still present in

Peter had already been calmed. Peter needed a long life, tossed to and fro, walking almost as profoundly through the abyss of guilt as Judas to finally be able to rest fully against the Lord's breast. All that makes him feel very close to us.

25. Why the Messiah is Also God's Servant

In retrospect, it is easy to say that Jesus Christ fulfilled the prophecy of the suffering servant of God. Isaiah says:

> He had no beauty or majesty to attract us to him, nothing in his appearance that we should desire him. He was despised and rejected by humankind, a man of suffering and familiar with pain. Like one from whom people hide their faces, he was despised, and we held him in low esteem. (Isa. 53:2–3)[1]

The last of the four so-called 'Servant Songs' describes the image of a martyred person who is so despised they are no longer tolerated by their community. This person is like Job, whose friends considered his suffering to be a punishment from God. The sin this person has burdened themselves with must have been great because their suffering is great. That is what Job's friends thought. But the prophet knows that this servant is innocent and suffers for us:

> Surely he took up our pain and bore our suffering, yet we considered him punished by God, stricken by him, and

afflicted. But he was pierced for our transgressions; he was crushed for our iniquities; the punishment that brought us peace was on him, and by his wounds we are healed.
(Isa. 53:4–5)

This is just what happened in Christ's Passion. But the fulfilment of Isaiah's prophecy in the events of Golgotha can only be diagnosed in retrospect. Who would have thought at the time that this tormented and reviled human being was at the same time the Messiah and Redeemer? Upon further reflection, we might ask: would Christ have become that despised person at all if the prophecy had been immediately related to him at the time?

Some passages in the Gospels and Acts make the connection. John the Baptist testifies to Christ with the words, 'Look, the Lamb of God, who takes up the sin of the world!' (John 1:29). And after Christ's death and resurrection, the disciple Philip enlightened a high state official from Ethiopia about the passage in Isaiah that speaks of the Lamb being led to the slaughter and exalted in death. Thus, the image of the Servant of God is blended into the image of the Lamb of God. Philip's preaching of the Gospel transformed the prophecy, so puzzling to the Ethiopian, into an immediate realisation of Christ's identity with the humiliated one. It prompted the man from Ethiopia to be baptised (Acts 8:27–39).

At various points, Christ announced his suffering and death in line with Isaiah's prophecy: for example, following Peter's recognition of him as the Messiah (see Mark 8:31, 9:31 and 10:33). At the anointing in Bethany, he said that the anointing would apply in advance to his burial (Mark 14:8). And then, of course, there are Christ's words at the Last Supper: 'This is my blood of the covenant, which is poured out for many for the forgiveness of sins' (Matt. 26:28).

25. WHY THE MESSIAH IS ALSO GOD'S SERVANT

These recall God's words about his servant in Isaiah, which are both so harrowing and so full of promise:

> And though the Lord makes his life an offering for sin, he will see his offspring and prolong his days, and the will of the Lord will prosper in his hand. After he has suffered, he will see the light of life and be satisfied; by his knowledge, my righteous servant will justify many, and he will bear their iniquities. Therefore I will give him a portion among the great, and he will divide the spoils with the strong because he poured out his life unto death and was numbered with the transgressors. For he bore the sin of many and made intercession for the transgressors. (Isa. 53:10–12)

Christ is the Man of Sorrows who innocently bears the people's sins and becomes their saviour through his suffering. Not only that, he was despised by those whose salvation he secured through his suffering. We also find it anticipated in Isaiah in a saying of the Servant of God: 'I offered my back to those who beat me, my cheeks to those who pulled out my beard; I did not hide my face from mocking and spitting' (Isa. 50:6). It is the picture of 'Ecce Homo', which Pilate displayed before the crowd: the tortured figure of Jesus of Nazareth, crowned with thorns, and for whom no reason could be found to condemn him (John 19:1–5). According to the Christian view, what was proclaimed in Isaiah is fulfilled here.

What is strange about all of this though, is that Isaiah's prophecy was fulfiled only because it was *not* accepted. Peter, for example, did *not* want to accept that Christ would have to suffer much, be rejected and killed. His understandable refusal to see the Servant of God in the Messiah led to the Messiah not being recognised. This in turn led to Christ's humiliation, the betrayal of the One of whom something quite different had been expected. They could not find the Messiah in the rejected one and were thus involved in the fact that he was rejected. To them, it was obviously impossible for the Anointed One to be so pitiful, and that was just why he became so. It seems as if the prophecy had to fall into unconsciousness ('...they know not what they do') in order for the mystery of sacrifice to be made effective as a power of destiny ('...yet not my will, but yours be done' Luke 22:42). The sacrificial power also lay in Christ's fully suffering the people's lack of understanding, who in turn also had to be forgiven for that very lack ('Father, forgive them, for they do not know what they are doing.' Luke 23:34).

In his humiliation, Christ bore the sin of the world. What is meant by this is not the simple fulfilment of a demand for compensation. The delicate concept of atonement or expiatory sacrifice is sometimes misunderstood in this sense of satisfaction, as if it were a matter of an offended God receiving reparations (Anselm of Canterbury advocated this view). The goal is not a balanced account, but rather it is the healing of humanity's relationship with God. This goes hand in hand with healing the human self.

Perhaps one could say that to bear the world's sin was about the principle of initiation that only came into the public eye with Christ's deed and could only then be recognised by all. It is about the principle of initiation, which, coming from a completely different cultural sphere, could nevertheless be recognised in Isaiah's servant of God. Admittedly, there is a danger here of reducing Jesus to the pattern of the great initiates. Therefore, the task is to escape the cliché by connecting the two religious spheres

25. WHY THE MESSIAH IS ALSO GOD'S SERVANT

– Judaism and Near Eastern mystery religions – and to recognise specifically how the highest and the lowest are united in that unexpected fulfilment of Jesus Christ's Messiahship.

Indeed, the highest is sublime only insofar as it is ready for full humiliation. The power of the ego lies not in its exaltation but in its readiness for powerlessness. With that power, Christ overcame what happened to human beings as a result of the Fall. He overcame the self-centred, ego-centred human nature, which is bent on self-preservation and self-enhancement, and which still comes to the fore in rejecting the idea that the Messiah could also be God's servant. Christ's suffering was about the birth of the true self for each individual human being. It was about a willingness to sacrifice that does not want to keep anything for itself. Through this, it finds its way into the true destiny and greatness of the self.

The Protestant theologian Oscar Cullmann posed the interesting question: 'At what moment in his earthly life did Jesus attain the certainty that he had to realise the task assigned to him as the *Ebed* (servant)?'[2] At what point did awareness of his mission as God's Servant live in him? Cullmann sees the key to the solution to this question in the 'heavenly voice' that Jesus heard at his baptism at the Jordan: 'You are my Son, whom I love; with you I am well pleased' (Mark 1:11). These words echo Isaiah 42:1, where they apply to *Ebed Yahweh*, the Servant of God: 'Here is my servant, whom I uphold, my chosen one in whom I delight.' According to Cullmann, Jesus acquired the consciousness of having to take on the *Ebed Yahweh* role at the moment of his baptism.

The baptism in the Jordan, familiar to us against the background of Rudolf Steiner's Christology, is the entry of Christ into Jesus of Nazareth. Here it appears in another illuminating light. With the baptism, not only does the Messiah enter into Jesus, but at the same time the Passion journey of the Servant of God begins. From that viewpoint, Christ's conception on Earth at his baptism also proves to be a path of pregnancy, which led to his birth through Jesus' death on Golgotha. The suffering of his incarnation preceded it.[3] Jesus was baptised into death at the Jordan by connecting the Messiah with the Servant of God. Cullmann points out that the voice of heaven at the baptism, along with the awakening of his consciousness of the Servant of God, answers the question that the first Christians asked themselves. If baptism takes place for the transformation and forgiveness of sins, what meaning did it have for the innocent one who came to the Jordan? John did not even want to baptise him, feeling instead that he was the one who needed to be baptised by the pure one. Jesus was not baptised for his sins but for those of the whole people. According to Cullmann, Jesus was baptised in view of his death. That was the mission of the Servant of God, 'that in his dying he would perform a general baptism on his people.'[4] Our task is to understand how the incarnation of God, which is at the same time a Passion completed only through human guilt, transforms our humanity.

26. Raising the Dead

Those who passed by hurled insults at him, shaking their heads and saying, 'You who are going to destroy the temple and build it in three days, save yourself! Come down from the cross, if you are the Son of God!' In the same way the chief priests, the teachers of the law and the elders mocked him. 'He saved others,' they said, 'but he can't save himself! He's the king of Israel! Let him come down now from the cross, and we will believe in him. He trusts in God. Let God rescue him now if he wants him, for he said, "I am the Son of God."' In the same way the rebels who were crucified with him also heaped insults on him. (Matt. 27:39–44)

Christ could prove to those who put him to death that he was the Son of God if he performed the miracle of saving himself from certain death. But that was just what he did not do. He did not perform a miracle but walked the human path through powerlessness into death.

But as his tormentors pointed out, he did indeed save others. Did he not perform the miracle of raising the dead beforehand, which proved his divine omnipotence?

There are three so-called raisings of the dead in the New Testament. When someone was brought back to life from death, at first sight, it seemed supernatural or magical, contrary to the laws of nature.

First, there was the revival of the young man of Nain, a story unique to Luke. On the way to the city of Nain, Christ and his disciples encountered a funeral procession carrying the 'only begotten son of a widow' to the grave. Christ felt great compassion for the woman because, as a widow, she was entirely without protection and sustenance due to the loss of her only son. 'Do not weep!' he said to her. Then he touched the coffin whose bearers stood still and uttered the words, 'Young man, I say to you, arise!' Thereupon the dead man rose, began to speak, and was returned by Christ to his mother (Luke 7:11–15).

Read in that way, this awakening appears above all as a miraculous act of mercy. It appears to happen less in the young man's interest than for the grieving mother, who would otherwise remain alone.

Rudolf Steiner, however, presented a completely different perspective on this event, one that was not concerned with Christ's omnipotence to perform miracles. Instead, it was directed toward the historical development of that young man to whom the call went out as an initiatory call: 'Young man, I say to you, arise!' This young man, according to Steiner, was in his previous life the youth of Sais. Like other initiates, he wanted to become a 'son of the widow', referring to the goddess Isis who mourned for her dead Osiris. In lifting Isis' veil in his hunger for knowledge, he had been hasty in striving for wisdom.[1] The shadow of this event lay over his incarnation in Palestine. Thus, he entered the sphere of death again at an age when the fully conscious spiritual life begins to set in. But there, through his encounter with Christ, he experienced a turning

26. RAISING THE DEAD

point in his destiny. That encounter sent him on a new path – one that led him to struggle with all seriousness for the new impulse that had come into the world through Christ.

According to Steiner, this individuality was born again in the third century AD as Mani or Manes, the founder of Manichaeism. The same individuality later incarnated in the Grail stream as the young Parsifal. Unlike the youth of Sais, who lifted the veil in a forbidden manner, Parsifal, partly in overcompensation, did not ask the critical question about the suffering of Amfortas, the Grail King. In the aftermath of that failure, however, through many journeys and struggles, Parsifal finally attained what he had once failed to achieve: the capacity for compassion within the framework of the Christian triad of faith, hope and love.

≈

The second raising of the dead that may seem like a miracle was that of Jairus' daughter. The girl, the only daughter of the synagogue ruler, was terminally ill when Christ was called to help save her.[2]

A crowd, who by then had witnessed Christ's healings several times, had surrounded him. Among them was a woman who had been suffering from the flow of blood for twelve years. She approached Christ in the sure hope that she would be healed if she could only touch his garment. Indeed, she was healed at that exact moment, while at the same time the daughter of Jairus seems to have died. At least that is what her father was then told. Christ's question of who had touched him at first caused the woman to fear and tremble because she was worried that she had done something wrong. Then immediately after her confession, he pointed out her extraordinary strength of faith, which had caused her to recover. It was just such strength that he then demanded of Jairus, who, together with Christ, was to awaken his daughter to a new life. She was twelve years old, beginning her marriageable life as a woman. She lacked the strength for that life. But then the strength was there – at the very moment of her death! It was present in a linking of individual destinies. There was too much life force in the woman who had suffered for twelve years, and too little in the twelve-year-old girl. Through Christ, these were brought into a harmonising relationship. The woman's unformed blood overflow and the child's anaemic stagnation of life balanced each other out.[3] Achieving that balance was the real miracle of this so-called raising of the dead.

The fact that we human beings are related to one another in our blood-bound selfhood is something we can understand quite well. We can try to understand the karmic relationships of the balance between the individualities, for example, in questions of guilt and suffering in the sequence of incarnations. But this double healing illustrates that we are also directly connected in this life. Our strength exists in relation to the strength of others. The healing involved the interaction of all those involved, including the woman's faith, that of Jairus, the presence of the parents, and three chosen disciples in Jairus' house. The special quality of balance, which cannot be implemented by the individual, but only in their relationship to other people and the common good, is the content of the mystery of that revival. It received its impetus through Christ's 'Maiden, arise!' The story itself was not under the sign of a supernatural raising of the dead, but under the sign of working together, without which the kingdom of God cannot exist.

≈

The most significant revival in the New Testament is the raising of Lazarus (John 11). Was Lazarus only asleep, or was he dead? There is a strong indication that he was dead when Christ finally

26. RAISING THE DEAD

came and wanted to know where he has been laid. In front of the tomb, when Christ commanded the stone to be rolled away, Martha, Lazarus' sister, said, 'Lord, by this time there is a stench.' Martha presumed the smell of decay that was expected after three and a half days in the tomb. Was Lazarus really dead? That seems to be the question here. The answer then makes Christ's act either a miracle or something entirely different, namely a new birth in the sense of an initiation, as we read in Rudolf Steiner.[4]

Against Martha's idea is the sentence Christ spoke right at the beginning when he learned of Lazarus' illness: 'This sickness is not unto death, but for the glory of God, that the Son of God may be glorified through it' (John 11:4). To take this sentence to mean that Christ's divinity would reveal itself by performing the miracle of raising the dead, would be to make Lazarus' illness and death an instrument for God's self-presentation. That idea corresponds to the world of thought promoted by the devil who tempted Christ to just such an act when he asked him to throw himself from the pinnacle of the temple to demonstrate that it could not harm him. Steiner counters this almost blasphemous interpretation of the Lazarus narrative with one that is Christian in the true sense of the word. The birth of a new spirit in Lazarus, the revelation of his divine being, was to happen in the crisis of Lazarus' illness.[5] When Lazarus died, his death was a birth. Lazarus became new. He became the one who was intimately united with Christ's life, death and resurrection so that he, the only male disciple, was able in the end to stand under the cross. He bore witness to all this in his extraordinary Gospel of John, of which he was the author.[6]

With his illness, Lazarus was on his way to becoming John. Christ waited two more days before leading him into his new life through his midwife's call, 'Lazarus, come forth!' It testifies to his allowing him the time needed for that transformation. Whether one calls that sleep or death is not decisive. Both are metaphors for the state immediately preceding the revelation of the divine in Lazarus.

That this event was misunderstood as a miracle is why some betrayed Christ to the Pharisees and chief priests. What does one do with a person who performs such signs and could thus make a Messianic claim that would seduce the people? Political prudence made the high priest Caiaphas consider, 'It is better for you that one man die for the people than that the whole nation perish' (John 11:50). From that day on, Christ's death was decided. But it is the great irony of history that, despite him, Caiaphas' sentence was fulfilled in a very different way from how he thought it would be. Christ died for the people and thus snatched them from ruin. The worldly misunderstanding became the catalyst for divine revelation and fulfilment.

27. Christ's Experience of Powerlessness

The incarnation of Christ did not happen on December 25 with the birth of Jesus in Bethlehem. It had its prerequisite there, but it only really began with the baptism in the Jordan and the entry of the Christ being into the corporeality of Jesus.[1]

In his lecture series *The Fifth Gospel*, Rudolf Steiner described the baptism in the Jordan as the 'conception' of Christ in earthly humanity. With that conception, a 'pregnancy' began that culminated in the 'birth' on Golgotha. That is, Christ was truly born on Golgotha and then lived his earthly life during the time between his resurrection and ascension and the subsequent outpouring of the Holy Spirit. He then entered the earthly sphere, just as human beings enter the world of the spirit when we die.[2]

Christ's incarnation was completed on the cross. There the supreme divine being experienced the powerlessness that we human beings are subjected to in death. Christ was truly human as the powerless one who fully experienced the human condition. Even though he turned it around in the resurrection, he first had to fully experience death, which had been part of human life since the Fall. But how could he do that as God? His powerlessness basically contradicted his divinity.

First, he could renounce power. That meant that he still allowed something other than himself to operate. Therein lies the basis for human freedom and the possibility that human beings can also turn against God.

But that was not enough. Part of the event of Golgotha and the incarnation of Christ is also that Christ encountered something that he had not simply *allowed*, but which he also suffered to some extent *involuntarily*. For all his willingness to take upon himself what was to come, he had to encounter something beyond his will. If he had deliberately wanted to become a victim it would, in effect, have made him an accomplice to a crime – that is, an accomplice to his own crucifixion. Christ became a victim of human beings in his death on the cross. His deed was to transform that violence and redeem those who brought him to the cross. That transformation of being a victim into the act of bringing a sacrifice is the liberating mystery of Golgotha.

Christ's Passion was an indispensable part of his incarnation. It was only fully a Passion if it also contained the moment of an experience of adversity. How are we to think that God encountered something that was not at his discretion?

~

At the beginning of Christ's incarnation, the adversary approached him and tempted him during his forty days of fasting in the desert. In principle, it made little sense to tempt God because, in contrast to human corruptibility, it was easy for him to withstand every temptation. But then, in Luke's Gospel, we learn that after Christ had overcome all the temptations, the devil 'left him until an opportune time' (Luke 4:13). An 'opportune time' when he would return. So did Christ not quite overcome the temptations after all? That cannot be said, for he neither turned stones into bread nor worshipped the devil to rule over the kingdoms of this world.

27. CHRIST'S EXPERIENCE OF POWERLESSNESS

Nor did he prove his divinity by throwing himself down from the pinnacle of the temple without being harmed.

Rudolf Steiner, completely in agreement with Luke referring to a return of the adversary, speaks of one of the three temptations as having an 'unanswered' or 'unresolved remnant', namely the temptation to turn stones into bread.[3] Steiner, unlike Matthew and Luke, positioned that temptation in last place. Christ could not be tempted on the level of arrogance – the dominion over the kingdoms of this world – nor by fear and pride – that is, falling into the depths unharmed. Those were temptations on the soul-spiritual level. The third temptation, however, concerned the material plane, where a god, so to speak, could not 'know his way around' at all. It was the temptation by Ahriman, the ruler of material laws.

Of course, Christ refrained from turning stones into bread. But he gave an inadequate answer: 'Man does not live by bread alone.' That is true, but people are nevertheless *dependent* on bread; we cannot live without it. Bread is existential. In it, we are subject to the laws of this world, and matter belongs to it. As a divine being, Christ did not yet recognise the significance of bread for humans in his own body, and it was just that ignorance that made him vulnerable. It was his Achilles heel.

It was Judas who would later lament the importance of bread. With him, the material conditions of being human announced themselves. Rudolf Steiner addressed that somewhat enigmatically when he said, 'Judas' deed was the question put by Ahriman that could not be fully answered.'[4] He did not elaborate, but there is a way of understanding this. The tempter, the adversary, did indeed come again in the form of Judas. The death-bringing betrayal that completed Christ's incarnation happened exactly where the stones-to-bread temptation is echoed a second time, namely in the anointing at Bethany.

In John's Gospel, it was Mary, Lazarus' sister, who anointed Christ's feet and head with precious oil. In Mark and Matthew, it was an unnamed woman in Simon's house. The woman was not sparing; she gave everything. The disciples complained about the enormous waste. In Matthew and Mark, it was all of them; in John, it was Judas who asked why that oil was not sold for three hundred silver coins and used to buy bread for the poor. From an earthly, human point of view, the woman's act seems like a senseless waste. Judas, who was particularly close to the money and managed the treasury, was horrified by this, so horrified that immediately after that wasteful action – as Matthew tells it – he went to the chief priests and asked, 'What are you willing to give me if I deliver him over to you?' (Matt. 26:15).

Judas, in his attachment to the earthly sensory world, fell prey to the temptation that Christ had all too easily overcome. Thus Ahriman, the adversary, returned. In the midst of the circle of his disciples, Ahriman turned against Christ, and so the figure of light encounters all the heaviness of the earthly-material. Since Judas could not sell the anointing oil and turn it into bread, he sold Christ, the Anointed One, and thus reduced the highest to the lowest. In precisely this way, however, God's incarnation was completed. He entered a realm of powerlessness beyond his control and thus, in a certain sense, involuntarily. Here the 'unresolved remnant' of the stones-to-bread temptation confronted him.

Christ's renunciation of power created the opportunity for an adversary to confront him. As a result, Christ suffered the death that befell him and became fully human. At the same time, however, he became the bread of life that transforms what it is to be human, for that death was the actual birth of Christ for the Earth.

In a certain sense, Judas turned stones into bread (namely, betraying Christ for money made from the mineral element, which

27. CHRIST'S EXPERIENCE OF POWERLESSNESS

could then be used to buy bread), but in a completely different way than Ahriman demanded of Christ during the temptation. An entirely different bread came into being, the bread of life. Judas thus became the catalyst of a great transformation. Unbeknownst to himself, Judas provided the conditions for matter to be able to spiritualise itself.

Christ had to submit to matter so that he could transform it. That came about through Judas.[5] But it was not planned that way. Both together make the Mystery of Golgotha possible, but also in that way, unpredictable. Only in the sphere of the unpredictable, in which something could still 'happen' even to God, does a true Passion take place.

There is another strange thing that should be pointed out here, namely the suspension of the usual chronology. At the anointing, when the disciples complain, Christ says, 'When she poured this perfume on my body, she did it to prepare me for burial' (Matt. 26:12). But that burial only happened because Judas took offence at the woman's sacrifice. Triggered by his offence at the anointing, only then did Judas create the conditions for the burial to which the anointing was supposed to apply.

This is a circular connection – Christ already knew what would happen, yet no one was predestined to do what Christ knew they would. Christ even fended off their reactions to the woman's actions: 'Leave her alone. Why are you bothering her?' (Mark 14:6). Here, the rational soul must capitulate to a higher temporal order and take the leap into the sphere of the spirit. Our categories of calculability – cause and effect, ends and means – fail here.

In Christ's death, which is the condition of a new birth, the deeds of both Judas and Christ reach their goal. Death was neither wished for nor intended by those involved. In the end, however, Judas' handing over of Christ coincided with the deed of God, who gives away his Son. The sacrifice, the self-giving of Christ, is the divine reverse side of betrayal. This is as monstrous as it is sublime. Divine tradition intersects with human tradition in such a way that with the betrayal, God's ultimate gift to humanity was fulfilled. And yet that was just how Christ became human and thus transformed humanity for all time to come.

28. The Transformation of Hell

> Why then do you wonder at the raising of Jesus? That is not what is to be wondered at, but rather the fact that he was not raised alone, but that he raised many others who were dead, who showed themselves to many in Jerusalem.

The above words are not found in the New Testament. They appear in the Gospel of Nicodemus (EvNik),[1] an apocryphal Passion Gospel written in the fourth century and probably supplemented in the sixth century by the so-called 'Descent of Christ into Hell' (chapters 17–27). They form the third part of the Gospel of Nicodemus, the 'Harrowing of Hell', which deals with the descent of Christ into the underworld. The descent also found its way into liturgy and Passion plays.[2]

This part begins with the above-quoted sentences of Joseph of Arimathea, who had asked Pilate for the body of Jesus to be buried in his tomb. In the narrative, Joseph had been imprisoned because he was a follower of Christ and had taken Christ's body into his custody. But he was miraculously released from prison without it being broken open, and even more astonishing was that the crucified one was no longer in the tomb but had been seen among the living. Joseph of Arimathea also brought up another issue: the resurrection of many other deceased who, in the meantime, could be seen among the living.

One of the main New Testament passages to which these phrases refer is found at the end of Matthew's Gospel:

> At that moment, the curtain of the temple was torn in two from top to bottom. The earth shook, the rocks split, and the tombs broke open. The bodies of many holy people who had died were raised to life. They came out of the tombs after Jesus' resurrection and went into the holy city and appeared to many people. (Matt. 27:51–53)

Dramatic natural events accompanied the great, world-shaking event of Christ's death. When God died, the earth shook. According to the vision, that earthquake opened the graves and awakened the dead. At the same time, Matthew seems not to want to anticipate Christ's resurrection, which is why he says that the deceased did not come out of the tombs until after Christ's resurrection. Taken literally, that led to the strange idea that those raised from death remained in their open graves from Good Friday to Easter Sunday before they came out. For us, this startlingly strange idea raises the question of what happened during this time, essentially on Holy Saturday. With the descent into Hell, The Gospel of Nicodemus, among others, seeks to give a pictorial answer to this very question.

To where did Christ descend? Matthew puts it this way: 'For as Jonah was three days and three nights in the belly of a huge fish, so the Son of Man will be three days and three nights in the heart of the earth' (Matt. 12:40). In the 'heart of the earth' does not sound like 'Hell' at all, but the term fluctuates in meaning.

Tradition knows a range of expressions for where Christ goes in his descent. In the Old Testament, for example, there is talk of

28. THE TRANSFORMATION OF HELL

Sheol, the dark place to which the dead go, both righteous and unrighteous. Hades is the Greek term for it. However, in addition to being the place for all the dead, it can also refer to where the 'wicked' dwell until the judgment at the end of time. Gehenna (the Greek-Latin form of the Hebrew Ge-Hinnom, a ravine near Jerusalem) goes more in the direction of a place of punishment for the ungodly, and Abyssos (abyss) denotes the place of imprisonment for demons (Luke 8:31). So, with the descent, we enter an underworld that fluctuates between a quasi-natural sphere of the deceased and a moral sphere for the godless.

The visions of the descent in the Gospel of Nicodemus tended to decide this tension in the direction of a more neutral realm of the dead, for there are no really morally reprehensible people to be found in that imagined underworld. Adam alone could be thought of that way because of his original sin. Otherwise, Abraham, Isaiah, David and John the Baptist all dwell here.

But this world is ruled by Hades – here thought of as a person. It was Satan who proudly announced his greatest 'catch' to Hades, namely, Christ, who had done Satan 'much evil' in the world above. By his mere word, Christ had healed the people whom Satan had made blind, lame and leprous, and he had brought back to life some whom Satan had killed. Now Satan wanted to render him harmless, and announced Christ's arrival to Hades who could keep him firmly in his power.

Hades, the Prince of Hell, however, was skeptical and not at all convinced that Christ's death and entrance into the underworld should be seen as a success. Indeed, he saw the danger for his kingdom, for he had recently experienced how Lazarus had been snatched from him. Whoever was capable of such a thing could actually only cause 'mischief' in the underworld. The Prince of Hell said to Satan:

> He is the same who took away from me Lazarus, after he had been four days dead, yet he brought him to life again by his power. Bring not, therefore, this person hither, for he will set at liberty all those whom I hold in prison under unbelief and bound with the fetters of their sins. (EvNik 15:20)

There is something almost amusing about how the underworld resisted Christ's knocking at its gates, and Satan dug his own grave in the belief that he had landed his greatest coup. Death resisted life. To secure his kingdom, Hades commanded his servants, 'Shut the brass gates of cruelty, and make them fast with iron bars' (EvNik 16:4). But it was all in vain. The Lord of Glory gained access, and all the dark corners of Hades became light. 'We have been defeated. Woe is us!' cried Hades.

Now Hell turned on itself, for Christ seized Satan, bound him in iron chains and handed him over to Hades – of all people – for safekeeping until his second coming (EvNik 18:14). Satan, a prisoner of Hades! 'In wanting to kill the Lord of glory, you have killed yourself,' said Hades to Satan (EvNik 18:9–10), expressing what Paul later said from a very different perspective: 'Death has been swallowed up in victory. Where, O death, is your victory? Where, O death, is your sting?' (1Cor. 15:54–55).

There is a salutary form of irony in the fact that he through whose temptation death entered the world was now himself under the spell of death. Hades himself summed it up when he said to Satan:

> Turn and see that no dead man is left with me and that all you gained by the wood of knowledge you have lost by the wood of the cross! ... In wanting to kill the King of glory, you have killed yourself. (EvNik. 18:9–10)

28. THE TRANSFORMATION OF HELL

This situation is depicted in the Anastasis (Resurrection) icon of the Eastern Church. Christ stands on the blasted gates of Hell and grabs Adam and Eve by their hands to pull them out of their sarcophagi (symbols of the underworld). Under the gates lies Satan, bound.

For the Eastern Church, Christ's journey to Hades and the resurrection are merged into one. It is not the empty tomb on Easter Sunday that indicates the resurrection but Christ's entry into the sphere of power of death, from which he liberates people.[3]

We know it differently. Let us think of the sentences of the Creed of The Christian Community: 'In death, he became the helper of the souls of the dead who had lost their divine nature. Then he overcame death after three days.' Christ's descent into the realm of death preceded the overcoming of death. The descent and the resurrection are two different things here, and yet there seems to be something like a transition between them. The Catholic theologian Gisbert Greshake says, 'By God himself entering the sphere of power of death, the latter ceases to be the zone of God's remoteness, of unrelatedness and darkness.'[4] Therefore, the connection with God is an overcoming of death, that is, a kind of resurrection. This is a metaphorical understanding of overcoming death.

In Rudolf Steiner's work, we now find yet another aspect of the descent's meaning – the enlivening of the beyond:

> This visit of Christ to the other world is hugely significant, and marks a revitalisation of life there between death and a new birth. At that important moment of the Graeco-Roman era, departed souls experienced themselves as shadows despite all their pleasure in the physical world, and would therefore have preferred to be beggars in the

upper world than kings in the realm of the shades. Since that time, though, they began to feel ever more at home again in the world beyond. Since then, too, people have increasingly grown into the world of the spirit, so that this moment marked the beginning of a period of ascent, of blossoming in the spiritual world.[5]

In these sentences, there is a new relationship between this world and the hereafter, between the world of the senses and the world of spirit. The realm of Hades is brought to life and, at the same time, the distance between earthly humanity and God is overcome in favour of a closeness to the spiritual world. The spiritual world blossoms. It is no longer a realm of shadows, an underworld, but the world of an ascent. For humanity, Christ's descent thus becomes an ascent.

29. Why Ascension Did Not Happen at Easter

Christ was not the only one who ascended to heaven. The mysterious figure of Enoch in the Old Testament also underwent a kind of ascension. His intimacy with God seems to have taken him from the Earth comparatively early, namely after 365 years, the full number of days in a year (some of his ancestors lived to be over 900 years old, see Gen. 5:3–32). 'Enoch walked faithfully with God; then he was no more because God took him away' (Gen. 5:24). The same is true of the prophet Elijah, who was taken up before the eyes of his successor, Elisha, by a fiery chariot with fiery steeds, riding with it in a storm wind towards heaven (2Kings 2:11).

But unlike Christ, neither Enoch nor Elijah died before their ascension. Both were caught up alive to God. They seem to have led their lives in such closeness to God that they had only a loose relationship with the earthly and the path to heaven was immediately obvious to them. Even in their earthly lives, they always belonged to heaven and were perhaps not fully incarnated.

Christ was different. He connected himself completely with the Earth and entered the density of the physical body, in which the forces of death had become stronger and stronger. Christ came to Earth to transform death through his own death. He died and was resurrected after three days, and only after another forty days did he ascend to heaven.

At least, that is what we read in Luke's Acts of the Apostles (Acts 1:9). In Luke's Gospel, however, the Ascension seems to conclude Easter Sunday (Luke 24:50–53). Nevertheless, many things happened before it. Christ appeared to the disciples at Emmaus and later to the other disciples when he ate fish.

Neither Christ's death nor his resurrection was his ascension. That is an extraordinary thing. Anything else would be easier to imagine, for both death and the resurrection could be imagined as an ascension into heaven. Indeed, there would hardly be a difference between death and resurrection, as death would then be the entrance into eternal life. That, however, would mean that the unique attribute of Christianity would be lost. Other religions that do not believe in a bodily resurrection nevertheless believe in an immortal soul. But Christianity also tries to avoid that problem by blurring the distinction between the resurrection and the Ascension for the sake of ease of thought, and equating Easter with the Ascension as the revival and exaltation of Christ.[1]

But it is not only about an abstract distinction but concretely understanding the significance of those forty days. Christ lived on Earth in his resurrection body and had conversations with his disciples about the kingdom of God.[2] Only through these forty days on Earth after Easter does the body gain the high esteem that cannot be found in any other religion's theology of the afterlife.

The body is the basis of Christ's connection with the Earth. Christ, like no other divine being, entered into a relationship with humanity through his incarnation. He related humanity to himself through his complete immersion in the earthly and through which he created the conditions for its transformation through his divine power.

29. WHY ASCENSION DID NOT HAPPEN AT EASTER

This connection with the Earth began with his baptism in the Jordan. There Christ, coming from the spiritual sphere of the sun, entered a human body. Rudolf Steiner uses the metaphor of 'conception' for the arrival of Christ on Earth. With this, a 'pregnancy' begins that comes to term with his 'birth' on Golgotha.[3] At that point Christ had permeated the physical body of Jesus of Nazareth right down to the skeleton. He shared in human mortality to the very last fibre of physical existence, and thereby transformed it into a new birth.

After his resurrection, he stood before Mary Magdalene, who did not recognise him at first. When she did she tried to touch him, but Christ strangely declared, 'Do not hold on to me, for I have not yet ascended to the Father' (John 20:17). Should she have been able to touch him after the Ascension? How could that have been possible? The passage will remain mysterious, but what can be gathered from it is that we are dealing here with a beginning in which there is a '*not-yet*'. Something has still to unfold, the beginning of a new process of growth. It had already reached the next stage when Christ – in contrast to the rejection of Mary – directly invited the disciples (Luke 24:39) and Thomas in particular (John 20:27) to touch him.

Once before we had to do with a first unfolding after a beginning, namely, when Jesus Christ was led by the Holy Spirit into the desert after his baptism. Here, too, forty days constitute an initial period of settling into a new existence. Symbolically, they allude to the forty years in the desert in which Israel was tested. At the end of those days were the three temptations. Christ underwent three trials. He was the 'challenged one' who had to prove himself in that new and strange state. Could he endure humanity without resorting to his divinity? If he had used his divine power at that time, everything would have been lost right at the beginning of his incarnation.

In contrast to the time Christ spent with the disciples after his resurrection, by going into the desert he entered into complete solitude. Then it was not yet a matter of his effect on others, not of communication, but of entering into the earthly body. Bodily existence is subjected to the conditions of hunger (stones to bread), power and greed (kingdoms of this world), and the childish desire for the miraculous (suspension of the effects of gravity). The adversary's temptations made him experience the special 'quality' of Adam, who went through the Fall.

We can observe some parallels if we relate these forty days and their temptations to the forty days after the resurrection. The episodes after the resurrection are more numerous throughout all the Gospels than Christ's three encounters with the devil after his baptism. Nevertheless, one can still identify very specific correspondences in which the tests are reflected in a completely transformed way.

Christ rejected the adversary's request to turn stones into bread. On the one hand, human beings are more than just beings who must eat (humans do not live by bread alone). On the other hand, Christ did not want to perform a miracle there. The post-Easter parallel to that test is found in Christ's request to his disciples to give him something to eat. At first, the disciples believed Christ's presence to be the appearance of a spirit. They did not want to believe that he was 'real' even after they had seen his hands and feet and had touched him:

> And while they still did not believe it because of joy and amazement, he asked them, 'Do you have anything here to eat?' They gave him a piece of broiled fish, and he took it and ate it in their presence. (Luke 24:41–43)

29. WHY ASCENSION DID NOT HAPPEN AT EASTER

At that point, it was no longer a question of dispensing with a miracle – the transformation of stones into bread – but of proving the truth of the resurrection to be real. But that reality was simultaneously of a different nature than the purely material. The resurrection corporeality was different than the materiality of the Good Friday corpse.

After his baptism, Christ was tempted to challenge God by throwing himself from the temple's pinnacle without dying. By renouncing this miracle, he consented entirely to becoming mortal. But after his transformation through Golgotha, he was genuinely present in a new corporeality. This was revealed in the fact that he could visit his disciples even when they were shut away in their meeting place (John 20:19). The body of the fallen Adam could not pass through walls; the body of the new Adam could.

Christ completely reversed the circumstances after the resurrection and effectively did what he refused to do for the devil in the desert. This also applied to that temptation in which the devil showed him the kingdoms of this world and said to him:

> I will give you all their authority and splendor; it has been given to me, and I can give it to anyone I want to. If you worship me, it will all be yours. (Luke 4:6–8)

There is an amazing correspondence between that scene and the end of Luke's Gospel. There Christ led his disciples out to Bethany and the Mount of Olives. He then lifted his hands and blessed them.

> While he was blessing them, he left them and was taken up into heaven. Then they worshiped him and returned to Jerusalem with great joy. And they stayed continually at the temple, praising God. (Luke 24:51–53)

The adversary's presumptuous temptation was not only rejected here at the end of the Gospel, as it was in the wilderness, but blessing and worship were proffered there in their proper place. Christ accepted the homage of the disciples, which he had refused the devil because it was due only to him. At the same time, he was, at that moment, lifted to heaven. In that way, he withdrew from the immediate encounters that had taken place in the previous forty days. That did not mean he 'returned' to heaven and was thus gone again. What he said at the end of Matthew's Gospel applies: 'And surely I am with you always, to the very end of the age' (Matt. 28:20).

Christ, however, does not have the oppressive presence of the devil. His ascension is about ensuring that humanity's newly emerging ego-consciousness is not robbed of its freedom by the self-evident and overwhelming presence of Christ.[4] He had to remove himself from physical sight so that human beings themselves could let him into their inner being. Christ wants to be sought by every human being. It is part of our post-Easter task to seek him out in freedom and let him in.

30. Pentecost

The Passover, which commemorates the Exodus from Egypt, is followed after seven times seven days by the Israeli Pentecost, the so-called Feast of Weeks. This feast commemorates the giving of the Law at Sinai. At the same time, it ended the harvest season, which had begun seven weeks previously. Thus, celebrating the outpouring of the Holy Spirit at Pentecost follows Christ's resurrection on the fiftieth day after Easter. The name Pentecost is derived from the Greek for fiftieth day (*pentēkostē hēmera*). After those fifty days, the coming of the Holy Spirit concluded Christ's work of salvation.

Something resoundingly new had entered the world with the first Passover. A new grain was harvested, and the unleavened bread of the new harvest took the place of the old sourdough. The enslaved Israelites could finally leave the land of their oppression because Pharaoh could no longer tolerate the tenth plague. All the first-born in his land fell victim to the angel of death, except the Israelites who sacrificed the Passover lamb. They were 'passed over' (*passah*, to leap over something, to leave untouched). Christ, who himself as the Passover lamb redeems all who turn to him, brought something into the world with his resurrection that was connected with both fear and joy because it could not at first be understood.

Nevertheless, it could be guessed that something decisive for humanity had taken place. It was a departure into the unknown, the new, which had entered into a first maturing after seven weeks. The disciples – including the women (Mary in particular) and Jesus' brothers – were 'joined together constantly in prayer' (Acts 1:14). They were gathered in a tense, expectant mood in which they knew that something was yet to come, but not what:

> Suddenly a sound like the blowing of a violent wind came from heaven and filled the whole house where they were sitting. They saw what seemed to be tongues of fire that separated and came to rest on each of them. All of them were filled with the Holy Spirit and began to speak in other languages as the Spirit enabled them. (Acts 2:2–4)

There had been seven weeks during which they had not truly understood what they had experienced on Golgotha and at Easter. And in the time between Easter and the ascension, they were in communion with the Risen One but still did not really recognise him. Rudolf Steiner speaks of a clouding of consciousness, of a state of sleep in which the disciples found themselves in the time leading up to Pentecost. Like sleepwalkers, they walked with the Risen One and could not grasp with their ordinary minds what they were experiencing.[1] Now the time had come; now they understood. The fiery tongues struck those present and they spoke in multiple languages.

No ordinary, earthly consciousness is capable of comprehending those things that came into the world with the death and resurrection of Christ. But through the outpouring of the Holy Spirit, the disciples entered into a comprehensively broad condition of consciousness, as indicated by their gift of speech that

30. PENTECOST

transcended everything individual. This had its significance not only as a new gift of perception but also for the presence of Christ on Earth in human beings. The 'subjective' or inner transformation of the disciples through Pentecost served as a sign for the 'objective' presence of Christ. The disciples awakened understanding created a new reality, which demonstrated God's need of humans for his existence on Earth.

The disciples' understanding at Pentecost was preceded by an incubation period characterised by a natural lack of understanding, which at least was aware that it lacked understanding. The epitome of the change in consciousness up to Pentecost was Peter. He fell asleep in Gethsemane at the hour of Christ's most severe affliction; he acted unwittingly during Christ's capture by cutting off a servant's ear, and then, completely unconscious, denied Christ three times. He was not present at Christ's death, and he also 'slept through' the resurrection, insofar as he was not the first to meet the risen Christ, though he is always named as the first disciple. Instead, it was Mary Magdalene. Finally, at the Sea of Tiberias, the disciple whom the Lord loved had to explain to him that Christ was standing there on the shore, telling them how to cast the net so they could catch fish. But as soon as he recognised him, Peter rushed to meet Christ and threw himself into the water (John 21:7).

As much as Peter was asleep, he awakened with Pentecost. He took the floor and delivered his Pentecost sermon, which went to the people's hearts so much that they asked what they should do. Peter answered them in a renewal of the Baptist's word:

> Change your mind and be baptised, every one of you,
> in the name of Jesus Christ for the forgiveness of your
> sins. And you will receive the gift of the Holy Spirit.
> (Acts 2:38)

Only with Pentecost did Christ come fully into the earthly sphere because he arrived in the consciousness of people who understood what had happened before. From this, we can also understand the idiosyncratic metaphor with which Rudolf Steiner speaks of the baptism of the Jordan as Christ's conception on Earth, of Golgotha as his birth, and of the ascension and Pentecost as his entering into the spiritual world the way human beings do at death. But unlike the transition into a spiritual afterlife following a person's death, for Christ, the Pentecost event meant expanding in the earthly sphere.

> Instead of entering a realm of the spirit, as human beings do after death, the Christ spirit brought a sacrifice by making its heaven on Earth, as it were ... The true sacrifice made by the Christ spirit was to leave the spheres of the spirit to live on Earth and among human beings, and thus give the impulse that would guide humanity and evolution on Earth towards the future.[2]

With Pentecost, Christ took up residence in the earthly sphere. With this, the deepest community of life with human beings became possible. He would not be ever-present in a dominating way, but as a real relationship, as something between himself and human beings. From that time on, human beings live in the nearness of Christ.

Philosophically speaking, the human being lives in the difference between self and Christ, which is the precondition for finding identity with Christ. The 'Christ in me', which threatens to degenerate into a cliché, can only be realised in that difference. It is also made real in our experience of insufficiency, in which we realise we have not yet arrived at that state of perfection but are on the way. This is the inspiration the Holy Spirit brings through the event of Pentecost.

It is a path of future development, of perfection. Each individual connects with the human principle of the Christ impulse. For that is the essence of the Christian Pentecostal idea: that everyone, no matter what country they come from and what language they speak, can nevertheless understand the principle of human community. It is togetherness in the spirit of truth and freedom. It is togetherness in the sense to which John testifies in Christ's saying, 'If you abide in my word, you are really my disciples. Then you will know the truth, and the truth will set you free' (John 8:31–32).

The figure of Mary, the mother of Jesus, has a unique and exemplary significance at Pentecost. She appears in many paintings amidst the disciples. She was the first to understand Christ and preceded the disciples in the Pentecostal inspiration through the Holy Spirit. For with the Annunciation, she had already understood what Peter understood only at the end; permeated by the Holy Spirit, she had known from the beginning. And just this connection through the inspiration of the Holy Spirit to universal humanity was what her husband, Joseph, found so alienating at first. He lived entirely in the context of his people, so he experienced Mary's pregnancy as unfaithfulness to his people's folk-spirit and therefore wanted to leave her. Only when an angel spoke to him in his sleep about the fulfilment of the Messianic prophecy through the Holy Spirit, was he able to take Mary completely to himself.[3]

Mary and Peter are the Pentecostal polarities that belong together: on the one hand, universal humanity, the readiness to serve the whole, the feminine side, and on the other, the individuality, drawn with clear strokes, the more masculine side. These unite in the spiritual event of Pentecost. A new law thus came into effect: the individual can only be free if they serve the whole. This is difficult because we face the challenge of overcoming our selfishness while at the same time not falling back on group affiliations. We are assisted in this task by the law of karma, which balances the developmental needs of the individual with the needs of humanity and brings the two into connection. We are also helped by Christ, who accompanies us throughout our earthly evolution, as he says: 'And surely I am with you always, to the very end of the age' (Matt. 28:20).

31. What It Means to Heal a Lame Man

According to Acts 3, a man who had been lame from birth sat in front of the temple in Jerusalem. For many years (he was over forty) he had known nothing but being dropped off there every day to beg for a living. When Peter and John went to the temple, it was the ninth hour, the time of the Jewish afternoon prayer. There they met the beggar. Peter, accompanied by John (who only appears here like an extra), turned to the man with an invitation, 'Look at us!' The lame man 'gave them his attention, expecting to get something from them.'

Peter then said to him, 'Silver or gold I do not have, but what I do have, I give you. In the name of Jesus Christ of Nazareth, walk.' Peter took hold of the man's right hand and lifted him up. His feet and ankles became firm; he stood up, jumped around, and walked into the temple with Peter and John praising God (Acts 3:4–8).

We are told about this healing at the very beginning of the Acts of the Apostles. What is reported there happened soon after Pentecost. The spokesman for the disciples at that time was Peter. He took on the task of proclaiming and explaining what had recently happened regarding Christ's life, death and resurrection, and he acted in the name of Jesus Christ. This 'in the name' characterised his work in this instance: Christ, not Peter, was the healer – Peter himself made that clear. He explained to the astonished and frightened people, the 'men of Israel', that they need not be surprised, for it was not he and John who had acted. Instead, it was 'the servant Jesus', whom the 'God of Abraham and Isaac and Jacob, the God of our fathers' glorified and whom those addressed there had put to death. But he had risen from the dead, and the healing that had just taken place bore witness to just that resurrection, which should convince the Jews.

This testimony seems to have been the apostle's primary concern. The lame man was healed for the sake of the proclamation. The atmosphere and gestures with which the lame man was healed were very different from those that had accompanied the corresponding healing by Christ. Indeed, Peter's healing had an air of unoriginality about it – or, if one wants to put it even more drastically, something of mere imitation. Somehow, it seems that what the Synoptics tell us about Christ's healing of the paralytic was to be repeated here.[1] Yet that healing had been both a physical healing and a deeper spiritual healing. The conditions for it were also given. In the Synoptics, the healing was based on a genuine and deep relationship to Christ. True, that was not stated directly by the paralytic himself but by those who brought him to Christ. Their trust in Christ was so great that they uncovered a roof to gain access to Christ, who was surrounded by many people. They lowered the paralytic on his bed through the hole in the roof. 'When Jesus saw their faith, he said to the paralysed man, "Son, your sins are forgiven."' (Mark 2:5).

A different spirit prevails in the healing of the lame man after Pentecost, subtly expressed in the gestures. The lame man looked at both apostles, expecting alms. His healing did not seem to be an issue for him. He did not even hope for it, yet he experienced it. The healed man ran and jumped, and of course he praised God

31. WHAT IT MEANS TO HEAL A LAME MAN

for the miracle, but there is no mention of his sins being forgiven as in Christ's healing of the paralytic. The healing that took place in Acts remained more external. It also included Peter's physical intervention, for he not only asked the lame man to get up and walk, but also helped him with his own hands. 'Taking him by the right hand, he helped him up' (Acts 3:7). There was none of that with Christ; no invitation to look at him, no action, no explanation, but the amazing sentence, 'My son, your sins are forgiven.'

Even though Peter's act was in the name of Christ, it seems in retrospect to have been Peter's will, for it allowed him to preach and explain to the men of Israel what had recently happened. That was what moved Peter, not the beggar's fate and state of mind in front of the temple. Peter was not concerned with the connection between faith and healing, which included the forgiveness of sins. He was concerned with the mystery of Christ's recent resurrection. It was that to which he witnessed in the healing that had just taken place.

But that was not the only thing to be proclaimed to the men of Israel. The sermon also contained a serious accusation concerning the one in whose name Peter performed the healing and which led to the central 'miracle' of Christianity:

> The God of Abraham, Isaac and Jacob, the God of our fathers, has glorified his servant Jesus. You handed him over to be killed, and you disowned him before Pilate, though he had decided to let him go. You disowned the Holy and Righteous One and asked that a murderer be released to you. You killed the author of life.
> (Acts 3:13–15)

Peter accused those to whom he spoke of murder, just as he did earlier in his Pentecost sermon, yet he also courted them. This was the time of church formation, of the development and growth of the Christian community. Peter proselytized and did so seemingly in the most inappropriate way imaginable. But the subject of this unconventional preaching belonged to a much greater miracle of healing than that which was performed on the lamed man, for the one whom the men of Israel had killed, God had raised from the dead: 'We are witnesses of this. By faith in the name of Jesus, this man whom you see and know was made strong' (Acts 3:15–16).

The healing of the lame man known to the city was proof of the resurrection of the one they had put to death. If they understood this, then they too would experience healing. That was a lot to ask. Peter was only willing to overlook what the men of Israel had done because they did it out of 'ignorance': 'Now, fellow Israelites, I know that you acted in ignorance, as did your leaders' (Acts 3:17). In the background, one hears here the dying Christ: 'Father, forgive them, for they do not know what they are doing' (Luke 23:34).

The real riddle is that the resurrection and its world-healing effect were preceded by the unknowing guilt of Christ's death. Only when we learn to deal with this without rationalising the evil deed as a means to the end of redemption (which is also redemption *from* evil) do we today have the prospect of understanding salvation. There is nothing that justifies murder, and yet here it has been done with salutary effect because it has been transformed. The men of Israel did not expect that transformation any more than the lame man expected his healing by Peter. That the one who expected money was graced with healing is extraordinary, just because the expectations were so completely different and completely undeserved. That healing, however, must subsequently be 'earned'. That is why Peter called

31. WHAT IT MEANS TO HEAL A LAME MAN

on his figuratively ill listeners, 'Repent, then, and turn to God, so that your sins may be wiped out' (Acts 3:19). It is just for that possibility of metanoia that Christ died and rose again. Peter, speaking to the Jews and following up on their previous history referring to Moses and the prophets, therefore said to them, 'When God raised up his servant, he sent him first to you to bless you by turning each of you from your wicked ways' (Acts 3:26). This ends Peter's sermon after the lame man's healing.

At the same moment, he and John were arrested by the priests and leaders, who were annoyed by their talk of the resurrection. Peter stood on very thin ice, and yet it held, for many of those who had heard him then confessed to what he had said.

In a comparable act by Paul, it is later clear how misunderstood healing can be. He, too, encountered someone lame from birth whom he wanted to heal. Unlike Peter's lame man, this one was deeply convinced of Paul's preaching of the gospel:

> Paul looked directly at him, saw that he had faith to be healed and called out, 'Stand up on your feet!' At that, the man jumped up and began to walk. (Acts 14:9–10)

Here, Paul's speech creates the prerequisite for a deep relationship, which was also evident in their eye contact. This lame man was completely involved; he participated in his healing. There was, however, a disastrous misunderstanding. While Peter spoke mostly to the Jews, Paul preached more to the Gentiles. Those who witnessed the healing by Paul could not explain it in any other way than that the gods had come down to Earth in human form. They wanted to worship and sacrifice to Hermes and Zeus, who they believed had appeared in Paul and his companion Barnabas. They were not to be imprisoned like Peter and John but wrongly worshipped. Thus, Paul wrestled not with the riddle of the suffering Messiah like Peter, but with the false gods of those to whom he wanted to preach the gospel. Either way, healing is a difficult birth.

32. Ananias and Sapphira: 'Why Has Satan Filled Your Heart?'

They were 'one in heart and mind' – so it says in the Acts of the Apostles about the first Christian community in Jerusalem (Acts 4:32). What united those people was that they were either eyewitnesses to the resurrection or heard about it from those who were. What united them in the spirit bound them together in the physical world. They lived in a community where they held all things in common, where those who had gave to those without so that none suffered from want (Acts 2:45, 4:34). They prayed together and broke bread with each other, they were part of the communion of the Lord's Supper, which was also for the vital need of being filled. Everything happened in great unanimity, where there was no lack, and even sickness was healed by the apostles. 'There is a magic in all beginnings,' one could say.

This spell, however, was greatly disturbed when a man named Ananias sold a field and lay part of the proceeds at the feet of the apostle Peter as an offering to the community. It's possible that he was motivated by Barnabas, who had also sold a field and given all the money to the apostles (Acts 4:36–37). This had made a deep impression on the community. Ananias probably wanted to achieve a similar effect without completely giving up his possessions, so he agreed with his wife, Sapphira, to sell some property in order to make a donation but to keep back some of the money and only pretend to give it all away.

Peter immediately recognised that there was something wrong with this good deed and said:

> Ananias, how is it that Satan has so filled your heart that you have lied to the Holy Spirit and have kept for yourself some of the money you received for the land? (Acts 5:3)

Peter pressed him further by stating that Ananias had not lied to the people but to God. That struck at the heart of the matter, and Ananias fell to the ground and died. Young men covered him, carried him out, and buried him.

Three hours later, Sapphira arrived, not knowing what had happened to her husband. In a mixture of interrogation and offer to hear her confession, Peter asked her, 'Tell me, is this the price you and Ananias got for the land?' She answered without hesitation, 'Yes, that is the price.' It was the critical question, a question that was supposed to reveal the woman's intentions and disposition.

Whereas Ananias had been somewhat restrained in his actions but otherwise silent, Sapphira now lied quite explicitly. She did not accept Peter's indirect offer to reconsider and describe how things had really been but confirmed the wrong deed with a lie. In doing so, she increased her husband's offense because, despite the chance to admit the wrong now that it had already happened, she persisted in the arranged deception, for which Peter then severely accused her. 'How could you conspire to test the spirit of the Lord?' (Acts 5:9) Sapphira also fell to the ground and died after Peter prophesied death to her. Whereas in the case of her husband, one could still assume that the lightning bolt of truth would cause him to give up his spirit in deadly self-knowledge,

32. ANANIAS AND SAPPHIRA

Sapphira seems rather to have been struck by the full force of God's punishment.

In both cases, 'great fear' overcame all those who learned of these deaths. In the case of Sapphira, however, Luke mentions that the 'whole congregation' was now afraid, and in doing so uses the word *ekklesia* for the first time – church.

That fear cast a shadow over the idyllic beginning of the community. We readers today certainly have a more challenging time with that shadow than the people of Luke's time because it has the taste of a threat. If you do not tell the truth, you will fall out of the community and be punished. And for what? After all, they were donating, but less than was admitted. Was the death penalty not exaggerated? Was not a God who behaved in such a way a despot?

With Ananias and Sapphira and the 'punitive miracle' performed on them, fear then entered the community. That fact made life in the community uncertain. They were no longer 'one heart and mind'. What had happened was not a trivial offense but something that could undermine life in the community at any time. It was not a matter of any 'donation laws' not being observed. There was no obligation to sell one's property and donate the proceeds to the community. Peter stated that clearly: 'The property was yours to sell or not sell, as you wished.' Also, after selling the field, Ananias could have used the money as he wished: 'And after it was sold, wasn't the money at your disposal?' (Acts 5:4). Ananias was quite free. And yet he was not.

The nature of the bondage to which Ananias and Sapphira had fallen was touched by the question that could not be so easily answered: 'Ananias, why has Satan filled your heart?'

The couple wanted to be like Barnabas, who had earned the congregation's recognition by his deed. That was the temptation – to appear pious and generous before the people.

It brought a status that flattered the self. But for Barnabas, who was attached neither to things nor money and did not want to appear more generous than he was, there was no longer any such temptation. He was already on the other side of a threshold, beyond possessions and prestige. From the beginning, Barnabas confronts us as someone who had arrived and been initiated. He could give everything, and it was not important for him to receive the appropriate recognition. He later became the advocate of the newly converted Paul (Acts 9:27), whom he accompanied on his missionary journeys (Acts 13 and 14).

But Ananias and Sapphira *were* concerned about such recognition and their correspondingly high reputation. At the same time, money was so important to them that they could not fully renounce it. If we look at their case with empathy, they too could have been people who knew that what really mattered was generosity and love for God and people. That was the distant goal that may even have shone forth for them. On the way there, however, they succumbed to the temptations of money and status.

And yet Peter's question remains tragically unanswered: 'Why has Satan filled your heart?' We can only conclude *that* Satan had filled the hearts of these two people, not why. He had filled them with the fatal twins of possessiveness and hypocrisy and had them firmly in his grip.

When those two soul powers appear together, they suffuse the fact of hypocrisy such that sin against the spirit lives in it. It was hypocritical to pretend to have a non-existent praiseworthy attitude, to keep the money but to pretend to have given everything for the life of the 'ones called out' (*ekklesia*). What's more, it affected all those who had come together to work towards the salvation of a community and each of its members. It can be compared to that beginning in paradise that was corrupted by the Fall. In each

32. ANANIAS AND SAPPHIRA

case, action sprang from selfish egoity. It is almost unavoidable, but nonetheless, precisely what was not supposed to happen.

Ananias and Sapphira exemplify the essential danger in which – to differing degrees – we all stand. For who can say that hypocrisy is altogether foreign to them? Who can say that their outward appearance is always congruent with their real self, and that they do not want to appear more and better than they are? Certainly, some modest people give as a matter of course and do so discreetly. We hardly have any knowledge of them just because their actions are hidden. But wherever modesty and devotion shine forth as a duty – as in the figure of Barnabas – at the same time, the danger of transgression is present. Dealing with that is the primary challenge, and in rising to meet it we are on the way to freedom, that freedom in which Satan can no longer fill our hearts.

Ananias and Sapphira are examples of lives lived in the tension between freedom and bondage, as expressed in Peter's question to Sapphira, 'Why then did you agree to tempt the spirit of the Lord?' It is clear that people cannot tempt God or lie to God. Why then did they do it? It was made even worse because they planned their deed together, and Sapphira's presumptuous hope that no one would notice their deception when she affirmed it afterwards was even greater. A change of thinking – *metanoia* – was not even considered.

In essence, she had judged herself and her husband, for in the end hypocrisy is its own kind of 'confession of faith'. It is the renunciation of the one who always knows, a renunciation of God, of conscience, of truth. 'Curse God and die,' Job's wife had said to her husband when she saw him suffering (Job 2:9). But Job did not want that; he maintained his spiritual integrity and thus his life and did so fully consciously. By contrast, Ananias and Sapphira gave up life and spirit needlessly and unconsciously.

Furthermore, that 'fall into sin' also affected the ideal community, which could no longer be as it was before. If everyone could behave like Barnabas, we would have paradise on Earth. But such a paradise cannot be created willingly. It is gifted to us. It is always dangerous for communities to try to create it themselves because there is the temptation to strive only for one's own well-being. Perhaps after the experience with Ananias and Sapphira, the congregation sensed just that danger. Perhaps they were much less afraid of the punishment for wrongdoing than of their own abyss – and of that question: 'Why has Satan filled your heart?'

33. Three Unlikely Baptisms

Stephen stood accused before the High Council because he proclaimed Christ and spoke critically about the temple and the law. Called to defend himself, he again criticised mere temple religiosity. God does not dwell in a temple built by human hands but in the open heavens, and he wants to be received by open hearts. As his accusers gnashed their teeth, Stephen had a vision of the Son of Man in heaven standing at the right hand of God. When he proclaimed this vision to them, his accusers lost control of themselves and stoned Stephen in an act reminiscent of lynching. Stephen died with the words, 'Lord, do not hold this sin against them!' (Acts 7:60).

This atrocity pleased Paul, mentioned here for the first time by his Jewish name Saul. Then, incited by what he had just experienced, he undertook a great persecution of Christians. Later, however, as we know, he would follow in the footsteps of the slain Stephen and preach the Gospel. This of all things, that the most zealous persecutor of Christians became the greatest proclaimer of Christ, surpassing even the effectiveness of Peter, is one of the most profoundly transformative events known to history. During Paul's conversion on the road to Damascus, he saw heaven open in a different, though no less intense, way than Stephen. It confirmed

Stephen's saying that the place to encounter God was not through the institution of the temple but through an inward receptivity to the divine light and to being addressed by God's Word. Paul was receptive because he was deeply serious about the true God. After the scales had fallen from his eyes and he regained his sight, he would be baptised (Acts 9:18). But before Paul's baptism, Acts tells us of two other baptisms that could not be more different. Indeed, the only quality they have in common is their improbability.

The first peculiar baptism after Stephen's death took place in the capital of Samaria. A man appeared, one of those seven who had been elected as ministers for the poor and confirmed by the apostles: Philip (Acts 6:1-6). He then proclaimed Christ. In contrast to the situation in Jerusalem, his word was accepted by all with one accord, and the signs he performed moved all who saw them: 'With shrieks, impure spirits came out of many, and many who were paralysed or lame were healed. So there was great joy in that city.' (Acts 8:7-8).

Fascinated by Philip's deeds, and presumably also by their effect on the people, a man named Simon also appeared in Samaria. He was a well-known magician in the city, who had so fascinated the people with his magic that they thought they recognised in him 'the Great Power of God'. Because of his miracles, he had been revered as a representative of God on Earth. But when the people now heard Philip's preaching of the kingdom of God and the name of Jesus Christ, they believed and were baptised. According to Acts, 'Simon himself believed and was baptised. And he followed Philip everywhere' (Acts 8:13).

Simon was amazed when he saw Philip's signs and great deeds. It may have been an ambivalent enthusiasm, for the magician encountered a man who seemed to have surpassed him in his own field. One might think that Simon had found a competitor

33. THREE UNLIKELY BAPTISMS

in Philip who threatened to steal his thunder, and yet it is said that he became a 'believer' and was baptised. Had he really been transformed because of that? Like Paul, who went from persecuting Christians to proclaiming Christ, had he gone from being a deceiver to being gifted with the Holy Spirit?

When the apostles learned that Philip could successfully preach the word of God in Samaria, Peter and John also came to the city to complete the mission there. They prayed for the people to receive the Holy Spirit and laid their hands on them, whereby the spirit did indeed inspire them. Simon also saw this and must have felt that such a gift of the spirit was not in his power. Therefore he offered the apostles money to tell him how to do it. In that way, he reduced the gift of the Holy Spirit to a magic trick.

Peter accordingly rejected him with sharp words:

> May your money perish with you because you thought you could buy the gift of God with money! You have no part or share in this ministry because your heart is not right before God. Repent of this wickedness and pray to the Lord in the hope that he may forgive you for having such a thought in your heart. (Acts 8:20–22)

Having just been baptised, Simon was immediately excluded from the congregation because he proved to be, in essence, only a sorcerer. He was a man who could produce what he wanted as an illusion and who was willing to pay for a pleasing outward appearance.

If baptism and the reception of the Holy Spirit normally went together, here they were separated. Baptism was followed by the gift of the spirit as a second stage. This stage made clear the whole seriousness of the conception of the spirit, willed from a person's innermost being. This passage in the Acts of the Apostles is the basis for the view of Confirmation as an affirmation of Baptism and as an independent sacrament. Simon denigrated the seriousness and truthfulness of his reception of the spirit through his offer of money.

And yet, at the same time, his case clarified that it was not a matter of external appearance. Here all illusions end: the magician would have to give up his profession if he wanted to belong to the kingdom of God.

But did he want to?

That remains unclear because his answer to Peter was ambiguous: 'Pray to the Lord for me so that nothing you have said may happen to me' (Acts 8:24).

He seemed to be agreeing to an act meant to secure his forgiveness more as a precaution. After all, he did not pretend to ask for forgiveness. In that respect, he renounced an illusion. And perhaps there was something to his becoming a believer and being baptised by Philip. Simon's ingrained profession was the creation of illusions – perhaps to the point that he himself could no longer distinguish between illusion and reality. How could he suddenly find a way out of all illusion and gain access to the truthfulness of baptism? How could he know whether his request for forgiveness was only about keeping himself free from harm or about a deep inner cleansing? It was almost easier to go from being a persecutor to being a preacher, like Paul had done, than from being a magician to being a true disciple. Here there is no clear contrast but a camouflaging confusion of consciousness. Metanoia is more endangered in the world of appearances than in the world of opposition.

The baptism of the Ethiopian that takes place between Simon's and Paul's baptisms, however, is quite different.

33. THREE UNLIKELY BAPTISMS

The angel of the Lord sent Philip, who had just baptised Simon, on the desolate road from Jerusalem to Gaza. On that road, Philip encountered an Ethiopian who, according to the understanding of the time, had come from the 'end of the world' to worship God in Jerusalem (Acts 8:27).

This man was the steward of the Queen of Ethiopia's treasure. He was a high official who dealt with money professionally but who was there on a very personal pilgrimage. He was on his way back to his country. On his return journey, he had nothing else on his mind but to study the Scriptures. He read the prophet Isaiah, and Philip asked him if he understood what he had read.

The Ethiopian sincerely confessed that he did not understand and needed guidance. Indeed, he had chosen a scriptural saying that was extremely difficult to grasp. It came from one of the Servant Songs and spoke of a man who was despised, considered to be afflicted by God, but who took our pain upon himself:

> He was despised and rejected by men, a man of suffering and familiar with pain. Like one from whom people hide their faces, he was despised, and we held him in low esteem. Surely he took up our pain and bore our suffering, yet we considered him punished by God, stricken by him, and afflicted. (Isa. 53:3–4)

Who was meant by this?

Philip explained to the Ethiopian that it was the Messiah, and that in Jesus of Nazareth he had suffered the fate foretold by Isaiah. The man must have had a profound experience, for, with noble determination, he pressed for his baptism immediately in a pond beside the road. With pragmatic matter-of-factness, Philip performed it. Philip had disappeared when the man came up out of the water, 'but he went on his way rejoicing' (Acts 8:39).

What is told here is improbable in many respects. The man came from another world; the road he took was remote, and he was a person who was constantly concerned with money. And yet, at the same time, he read the most difficult passages in Scripture. But all that detail was only the background for his strong will to find his way to God. Unlike the magician, who had to find his way out of his entanglement with money and illusion, here we have a completely truthful man for whom, however, the external conditions made baptism seem almost impossible.

This even applied to his physical condition. This man was an official and a eunuch; he was not a circumcised Jew, but a castrated Gentile. In Israel, such people, who could not live on in their descendants, were excluded from temple worship: 'No one who has been emasculated by crushing or cutting may enter the assembly of the Lord.' (Deut. 23:1–2). The Ethiopian found his way into a very different temple, the one Stephen had meant when he spoke of the Risen One and his congregation. In that temple, those who had been cut are also accepted. The Ethiopian was the first Gentile to become a Christian. He thus stands with Simon and Paul in a memorable line of baptised persons.

Endnotes

1. Herod and Nimrod: Hinderers Who Can Prevent Nothing
   1. Steiner, *The Gospel of Matthew*, lecture of September 3, 1910.
   2. Gorion, *Die Sagen der Juden: Die Erzväter* [Legends of the Jews: The Patriarchs].

2. At the Well: Hagar and the Angel; Rebekah and Isaac; Rachel and Jacob; Joseph
   1. Frieling, *The Complete Old Testament Studies*, p. 134f.
   2. Mann, Thomas, *Joseph and His Brothers*, Everyman, UK 2005.

3. Joseph: How Dreams Come True
   1. Mann, Thomas, *Joseph and His Brothers*.
   2. See Bock, *Genesis*, for a different explanation of the brothers' decision to expel Joseph. See also Steiner, *Deeper Secrets of Human Evolution in the Light of the Gospels*, lecture of November 14, 1909, for Joseph's role in reviving Egypt's impoverished intellectual thinking.

5. Moses and His Mission: On the Way to Selfhood
   1. Rienecker, Fritz (ed.), *Lexikon zur Bibel*, [Lexicon for the Bible], see entry for 'Moses'.
   2. Moses' journey on the Nile in the seclusion of the basket can, in my opinion, be explained with some interpretive force as an initiation in a kind of coffin. Why should one initiate an infant? See Emil Bock's *Moses* with slight reference to Rudolf Steiner.
   3. Steiner, *Turning Points in Spiritual History*, p. 127.

6. Moses Does Not Enter the Promised Land
   1. Bock, Emil, *Moses*, p. 122.
   2. Ibid., p. 123.
   3. Ibid., p. 130.

7. Rahab: Preparing the Way
   1. Archaeological excavations have shown that Jericho had long since been destroyed and no longer existed at the time of the 'taking of the land'.

This once again raises the question of the meaning and intention of the narrative. See www.bibelwissenschaft.de/wibilex/dasbibellexikon/lexikon/sachwort/anzeigen/details/rahab

2. See Chapter 23: Christ and the Samaritan Woman.

12. Job: The Rebellious Sufferer

1. Türcke, Christoph, *Umsonst leiden, Der Schlüssel zu Hiob*, [Suffering in Vain, The Key to Job], Dietrich zu Klampen, Germany 2017, p. 46.
2. Ibid., p. 47.

13. Judith: Pious Liberator or Temptress?

1. See Schmitz, Barbara, 'Trickster, Schriftgelehrte oder femme fatale? Die Juditfigur zwischen biblischer Erzählung und kunstgeschichtlicher Rezeption' [Trickster, Scribe or Femme Fatale? The Judith Figure between Biblical Narrative and Art Historical Reception] in *Biblisches Forum* [Biblical Forum].
2. Schmitz, op. cit.

14. Jonah the Initiate: Three Days in the Fish

1. See Ewertowski, Ruth, *Revolution im Ich. Einweihung als Wiedergeburt in Anthroposophie und Literatur* [Revolution in the Ego. Initiation as Rebirth in Anthroposophy and Literature].
2. See Steiner, *Christianity as Mystical Fact*, Chapter 7: The 'Miracle' of Lazarus.
3. Bock, Emil, *Kings and Prophets*, p. 231.

16. Daniel: A Loyalty Beyond the Reach of Power

1. Emil Bock considers it possible that the fourth figure in the furnace is Daniel, who need not be so different from a guardian angel-like spirit.

17. Dreams Change When Christ Appears

1. One such critical voice belongs to the prophet Jeremiah (Jer 23:25–28).

18. Mary and Elizabeth

1. Steiner, *The Gospel of St Luke*, p. 103.
2. Ibid., p. 92.
3. See also the wonderful essay by Hella Krause-Zimmer: 'Wiederverkörperung des Adam. Jesus and the Baptist' [Re-embodying Adam. Jesus and the Baptist], in *Anthroposophie. Mitteilungen aus der anthroposophischen Arbeit in Deutschland* [Anthroposophy. Communications from anthroposophical work in Germany], 1988, issue 3.

4. Steiner, *From Jesus to Christ*, p. 138.
5. Steiner, *The Gospel of St Luke*, p. 104.
6. See Steiner's *The Gospel of Luke*, lecture of September 26, 1909, for his view on the concept of 'virgin birth'.

19. The Birth of Jesus: Uniquely Atypical

1. Thus we find in a commentary on the Gospel of Luke at the time of Rudolf Steiner the following statement: 'But the existence of a completely different one in Matthew ... speaks against the historicity of Luke's narrative of childhood.' See Erich and Hugo Gressmann, *Das Lukasevangelium: Band 2*, Handbuch zum NT, [The Luke Gospel – Handbook to the New Testament: Volume 2), Germany 1919, p. 365.
2. Steiner, *The Gospel of Luke*, see lecture of September 16, 1909.
3. Steiner, *The Bhagavad Gita and the West*, see lecture of January 1, 1913.

20. Moses and John: The Tragedy of the Forerunners

1. Moses differed from other prophets in that he was a spokesman and messenger of God rather than one who knew and proclaimed what was coming.
2. According to Rudolf Steiner, however, John the Baptist remained connected with the twelve apostles after death with his highly developed powers of conscience and moved into Lazarus' individuality when the latter was raised from the dead. On these connections, see Sergei Prokofieff, *The Mystery of John the Baptist and John the Evangelist at the Turning Point of Time*, Temple Lodge, May 2005.

21. Appearances of God

1. Steiner, *The Principle of Spiritual Economy*, p. 93.
2. Selg, Peter, *Epiphanias, Fest der Geisttaufe* [Epiphany, Feast of the Baptism of the Spirit], 2nd edition, Stuttgart 2019, p. 25f.
3. Compare the rendition of the Gnostic Kerinthos (born around AD 100) by Irenaeus of Lyon: 'Jesus was not born of a virgin, but was the son of Joseph and Mary, begotten like the rest of men, but surpassing them all in righteousness, prudence and wisdom. After his baptism, Christ descended on him from the sublime primal principle in the form of a dove, and then he preached the unknown Father and accomplished mighty things; but in the end Christ departed from Jesus again, and Jesus suffered and rose from the dead. Christ, however, was spared suffering because he was spiritual' (Irenaeus of Lyons: *Contra Haereses*, I 26,1).

22. Nicodemus: On the Threshold of a New Birth
1. See Steiner's *The Gospel of St John and Its Relation to the Other Gospels*, lecture of July 3, 1909, for his explanation of the phrase 'by night'.

23. Christ and the Samaritan Woman
1. Voigt, Gottfried, *Homiletische Auslegung der Predigttexte. Die bessere Gerechtigkeit* [Homiletic Interpretation of Sermon Texts. The Better Justice], Spenner Hartmut, Germany 2005, p. 105.
2. Rudolf Steiner understands the sixth man as the spirit self, which must be developed in the future. The other five men stand for the underlying members of the human being. See Rudolf Steiner, *True Knowledge of the Christ*, lecture of November 21, 1907.

24. Simon Peter: Courage and Weakness
1. See Steiner's *The Gospel of Mark*, lecture of September 20, 1912, for his interpretation of the parallel passage in Mark of 'Get thee behind me, Satan!'

25. Why the Messiah is Also God's Servant
1. Since the end of the seventeenth century, the anonymous author of chapters 40–55 of the book of Isaiah, in which the so-called Servant Songs are found, has been called 'Deutero-Isaiah' (from the Greek meaning 'second Isaiah'). For various reasons these chapters can only be the work of a younger author who cannot be identical with the author of the preceding chapters. For chapters 56–66 one assumes a 'third Isaiah' ('Trito-Isaiah') or several other authors.
2. Cullmann, Oscar, *Die Christologie des Neuen Testaments*, [The Christology of the New Testament] Tübingen 1957, p. 65.
3. On the metaphor of 'conception' at the baptism of the Jordan and 'birth' on Golgotha, see Steiner, *The Fifth Gospel*, lecture of October 3, 1913.
4. Cullman, op. cit. p. 66.

26. Raising the Dead
1. On the individuality of the young man at Nain and his successive incarnations, see Rudolf Steiner, *From the History and Contents of the First Section of the Esoteric School*, pp. 194–96. See also *The Gospel of St Luke*, lecture of September 26, 1909.
2. Matt. 9:18–26; Mark 5:22–43; Luke 8:41–55.
3. Rudolf Steiner comments on this double healing several times. See, for example, *Building Stones for an Understanding of the Mystery of Golgotha*, lecture of April 10, 1917.

4. See Steiner *Christianity as Mystical Fact*, Chapter 7: The 'Miracle' of Lazarus.
5. Ibid.
6. Incidentally, this observation of Steiner's is not found in *Christianity as Mystical Fact* (originally published in 1902), but only later in the lectures on the Gospel of John (given in 1906/07). See also *True Knowledge of the Christ*, lecture of November 20, 1907.

27. Christ's Experience of Powerlessness
1. See *Die Christengemeinschaft*, issue 1/2016, p. 10f.
2. Steiner, *The Fifth Gospel*, lecture of October 3, 1913.
3. Ibid., lecture of December 10, 1913; see also lectures of October 5 and November 18, 1913, in the same volume.
4. Ibid., p. 133.
5. See Ewertowski, Ruth, *Judas. Das Paradox von Schuld und Sinn*, [Judas, the Paradox of Guilt and Meaning], chapter 'Vom Sinn des Verrats' [The Meaning of Betrayal].

28. The Transformation of Hell
1. (https://www.sacred-texts.com/bib/lbob/lbob10.htm)
2. Thus the phrase 'descended into Hell' found in the Apostles' Creed and the Redentin Easter play, goes back to the descent into Hell described in the Gospel of Nicodemus.
3. Gietenbruch, Felix: *Höllenfahrt Christi und Auferstehung der Toten, Ein verdrängter Zusammenhang* [Christ's descent into Hell and resurrection of the dead, a repressed connection], Germany 2010.
4. Greshake, Gisbert, 'Auferstehung' [Resurrection], in: Christian Schütz (ed.), *Praktisches Lexikon der Spiritualität* [Practical Dictionary of Spirituality], Herder, Germany 1992.
5. Steiner, *Disease, Karma and Healing*, p. 37f.

29. Why Ascension Did Not Happen at Easter
1. Conzelmann, Hans, *Grundriss der Theologie des Neuen Testaments* [Outline of the Theology of the New Testament], 4th ed., Tübingen 1987, p. 49.
2. According to Rudolf Steiner, in these conversations Christ taught his disciples in an esoteric way, among other things, about the four mystery chapters that later entered the mass. See *The Sun Mystery*, lecture of April 13, 1922.
3. Steiner, *The Fifth Gospel*, lecture of October 3, 1913.
4. Steiner, *The Mystery of the Trinity*, lecture of July 30, 1922.

30. Pentecost
    1. Steiner, *The Fifth Gospel*, lecture of October 2, 1913.
    2. Steiner, *The Fifth Gospel*, p. 31f.
    3. Steiner, *The Festivals and Their Meaning*, p. 254f.

31. What It Means to Heal a Lame Man
    1. Matt. 9:2–7; Mark 2:1–12; Luke 5:17–26.

Bibliography

Bock, Emil, *Childhood of Jesus*, Floris Books, UK 2014.

—, *Genesis*, Floris Books, UK 2011.

—, *Kings and Prophets*, Floris Books, UK 2006.

—, *Moses*, Floris Books, UK 2011.

Ewertowski, Ruth, *Judas. Das Paradox von Schuld und Sinn* [Judas: The Paradox of Guilt and Meaning], Urachhaus, Germany 2019.

—, *Revolution im Ich. Einweihung als Wiedergeburt in Anthroposophie und Literatur* [Revolution in the Ego. Initiation as Rebirth in Anthroposophy and Literature], Freies Geistesleben, Germany 2010.

Frieling, Rudolf, *The Complete Old Testament Studies*, Floris Books, UK 2022.

Gorion, Micha Josef bin, *Die Sagen der Juden: Die Erzväter* [Legends of the Jews: The Patriarchs], Literaricon Verlag, Germany 2023.

Prokofieff, Sergei, *The Mystery of John the Baptist and John the Evangelist at the Turning Point of Time*, Temple Lodge, UK 2005.

Selg, Peter, *Epiphanias, Fest der Geisttaufe* [Epiphany: Festival of Spirit Baptism], Ita Wegman Institute, Germany 2019.

Steiner, Rudolf, *The Bhagavad Gita and the West* (CW 142/146), SteinerBooks, USA 2009.

—, *Building Stones for an Understanding of the Mystery of Golgotha* (CW175), Rudolf Steiner Press, UK 2015.

—, *Christianity As Mystical Fact* (CW8), SteinerBooks, USA 2006.

—, *Deeper Secrets of Human Evolution in the Light of the Gospels* (CW117), Rudolf Steiner Press, UK 2021.

—, *Disease, Karma and Healing: Spiritual-Scientific Enquiries into the Nature of the Human Being* (CW10), Rudolf Steiner Press, UK 2013.
—, *The Festivals and Their Meaning*, Rudolf Steiner Press, UK 1996.
—, *The Fifth Gospel: From the Akashic Record* (CW148), Rudolf Steiner Press, UK 1995.
—, *From Jesus to Christ* (CW131), Rudolf Steiner Press, UK 1991.
—, *From the History and Contents of the First Section of the Esoteric School: Letters, Documents and Lectures – 1904–1914* (CW264), Steiner Books, USA 2011.
—, *The Gospel of St John and Its Relation to the Other Gospels* (CW112), Anthroposophic Press, USA 1982.
—, *The Gospel of St Luke* (CW114), Rudolf Steiner Press, UK 1988.
—, *The Gospel of St Mark* (CW139), Anthroposophic Press, USA 1986.
—, *The Gospel of St Matthew* (CW123), Rudolf Steiner Press, UK 1965.
—, *The Mystery of the Trinity* (CW214), SteinerBooks, USA 2016.
—, *The Occult Truths of Myths and Legends* (CW92), Rudolf Steiner Press, UK 2022.
—, *The Principle of Spiritual Economy* (CW109), Anthroposophic Press, USA 1986.
—, *The Sun Mystery and the Mystery of Death and Resurrection* (CW 211), SteinerBooks, USA 2006.
—, *True Knowledge of the Christ* (CW100), Rudolf Steiner Press, UK 2015.
—, *Turning Points in Spiritual History*, SteinerBooks, USA 2007. (Contains a selection of lectures taken from GA60 and GA61).

Websites

The Gospel of Nicodemus:
   https://www.sacred-texts.com/bib/lbob/lbob10.htm.

For news on all our **latest books**, and to receive **exclusive discounts**, **join** our mailing list at:

florisbooks.co.uk/signup

Plus subscribers get a FREE book with every online order!

We will never pass your details to anyone else.

www.ingramcontent.com/pod-product-compliance
Lightning Source LLC
Chambersburg PA
CBHW072050110526
44590CB00018B/3114